LIBERATING CHRISTIAN LEARNING

A HANDBOOK FOR LEADERS & FACILITATORS

RHONA KNIGHT, SALLY MYERS AND SALLY NASH

Cover page image: Wild Geese by Karen Herrick, Harlequin Arts.
Used by permission.

About the authors:

Revd Dr Rhona Knight was a GP and medical educator for over 25 years. Prior to ordination she led the Royal College of General Practitioners educational programme to enable medical practitioners to promote flourishing in healthcare. After ordination, she worked in theological education. She has a number of publications covering various areas. Now retired, she is researching trauma in ministry and also teaches and enables learning in areas of practical theology, including spirituality, flourishing and boundaries in ministry. She continues as a pastoral supervisor, spiritual accompanier and retreat leader. She can be contacted at revrhona@btinternet.com.

Revd Dr Sally Myers is a theological educator and researcher with over thirty-five years' experience in leadership roles. Her interests are centred around how we represent our faith to ourselves and others, and how those representations transform over time in response to life, learning and listening. She has a particular passion for encouraging and enabling flourishing in faith and making sure resources that support this are accessible and relevant to all. Her current role is Director of Focal Ministry in the Diocese of Sheffield. She is also Visiting Lecturer and Visiting Senior Research Fellow at Bishop Grosseteste University. She can be contacted at sally.myers@cantab.net.

Revd Dr Sally Nash is now a freelance theological educator, author, consultant, mentor, researcher and spiritual accompanier, having spent over forty years in some form of education and training including work with Youth for Christ and at St John's College, Nottingham. She is a Senior Fellow of the Higher Education Academy and a qualified school teacher. Her current roles include being Senior Research Fellow at St Padarn's Institute, Cardiff, Research and Training Lead for the Centre for Paediatric Spiritual Care and Associate Minister at Hodge Hill Chur in Birmingham. She is a practical theologian and has published on a wide rang ministry related issues and her current foci are shame and longevity in mir She blogs regularly at https://markerpostsandshelters.wordpress.com/, be connected with on LinkedIn and Facebook. She can be con revsally12@gmail.com.

Table of Contents

Foreword

Something new is stirring in the church. It's related to the rediscovery of the language of discipleship and its connection to lifelong learning. So every baptised Christian of whatever age is a learner. And the church is a community of learners who together are being formed into the likeness of Christ. There are no experts in this community because everyone learns from each other as the Holy Spirit moves between us.

First and foremost, therefore, disciples are called to learn from Jesus Christ and be open to all that the Holy Spirit wants to give us. This is an active process which requires that we learn how to learn. So, there is a growing realisation that this involves each of us understanding ourselves and our unique personality and how this then shapes our approach to learning. It also involves developing habits of reflective practice, spiritual direction or accompaniment, and finding a mentor or coach.

Liberating Christian Learning is an immensely practical book which interweaves theories of learning with real life examples. I would recommend reading it, first and foremost, for your own learning, i.e. with the questions, 'how do I learn?' and 'what practices do I need to develop in order to learn more?' Only secondly should it be read with a view to teaching. For as Knight, Myers, and Nash point out, those called to the specific ministry of teaching are more facilitators and curators than sages and lecturers. All good teaching comes out of our own learning, so that we are not just teaching other people's theories, but rather, that which we have found to be true in our own lives.

So whether you are just starting out as a Christian learner, or whether you have spent so many years learning that you have discovered just how much more there is to learn, I recommend this book as a companion on the journey.

Rt Revd Martyn Snow, Bishop of Leicester

Introduction

The idea of leading a group of Christians in learning more about their faith can be pretty daunting. In fact, if you do not feel even a little bit nervous then you probably haven't thought about it properly! However, it is also a great privilege, and with a bit of guidance, encouragement and a few checklists, great fun. This book offers a basic introduction to this great calling. It brings together theory and practice, with an emphasis on the practical. It offers checklists and top tips together with examples of what might go wrong and how not only to survive these inevitable events, but turn them into learning opportunities. The aim is to present a whistle-stop tour of adult Christian learning. We will introduce each topic as simply as possible and in the course of the book we will suggest various resources for those wanting to follow up various themes in more detail.

Part of what we hope to do when we lead learning is to encourage people to realise that we are all lifelong learners. This requires an attitude of humility in the leader and the will to create the right environment for people to flourish. It is also about learning holistically and gently growing in wisdom as the Bible talks about Jesus doing (Luke 2.52). When we think about different dimensions of learning, therefore, we want to consider how what we offer helps people grow in their knowledge, but also in their spirituality, service and vocations. We are called to love God with all our heart, soul, strength and mind, and our learning includes all of these. Embodied learning develops our ability to serve God and one another, whether through acquiring particular skills in pastoral visiting, prayer, swinging a thurible or theology.

If you have not guessed it from the title, this book is written from a particular perspective and with a particular view of education and faith: that of liberation. There are many different people writing about this and we are especially conscious of our white western background. We hope any assumptions made in ignorance will be forgiven. Our motivation in writing, teaching and prayer is simply to try to help release people from fear, ignorance and oppression. As facilitators of learning we aim to recognize, affirm and encourage people in using their emergent and dormant gifts for building up the Kingdom of God. Not everyone thinks about faith and education in the same way though, and to illustrate this we begin with some light-hearted fictional caricatures which outline different motivations and approaches. (Any resemblance to real people is probably inevitable!)

Sage

Sage, a member of a medium-sized church, was very surprised to be asked to oversee this year's Lent course. No one had asked them to do more than make tea for years! Perhaps someone had found out they spent 30 years as the national training lead for a massive government department before they retired. They could just about remember this, but were extremely nervous nevertheless. They knew that the subject, people and place were completely different and so they needed to think things through very carefully. They began by setting aside a regular time to pray about it all.

As they prayed, one by one, different individuals and groups of people came into their mind: the harassed single parent, the newly-weds, the pastoral visiting team, the over 50s group (well-over!), the choir, the visitors to the food bank, the office manager who comes to sit quietly in the church at lunchtimes, the shy teenage computer programmer. After a while they had to extend the time they spent praying because there were simply so many. What would these people really want to learn about their faith they wondered? There was no point in second guessing and so they decided to ask.

They asked the question on different social media. They also pinned a poster on the notice boards of all of the different places they could think of, and provided a blank piece of paper and a telephone number for people to respond. After a while they collected up the replies.

Some of the answers were a bit rude, but others were really interesting and many were heartfelt. There were of course many different themes but Sage was able to identify some themes that were quite close to the recommended Lent Book that year. They chose five themes to tailor the material to and made a careful note of the others for future reference. Sage then prayed about where and when to hold the sessions.

There had to be access and room for everyone who turned up. Also, they had to feel comfortable and, of course, be able to get there in the first place. In the end Sage decided to deliver the sessions twice each week, once in the afternoon in the Church Hall and once in the local school in the evening. At this point Sage thought it would be great to get some other people involved and so prayed some more and then asked people from the various groups if they would mind helping in whatever way they felt comfortable. This proved a great idea.

In no time at all there were people offering to help provide refreshments, lifts, babysitting, facilitating group work on individual tables and IT support that involved things Sage had not even heard of: apparently (provided consent was given by those involved) the sessions could be put into bitesize chunks and accessed for free, worldwide.

The evening was of course begun in prayer. To be honest, it was a bit chaotic. The children continued playing and a baby cried until it found its mother's breast. Some of the older people couldn't hear and so the sound had to be adjusted. However, no one seemed to mind at all, because they were relaxed and able to be themselves, and there was a wonderful spirit among them. People asked lots of questions about things that had been bothering them for years, and at the end, everyone seemed pleased.

Skyler

Skyler, a curate at a medium-sized church, was asked by their training minister to take responsibility for this year's Lent Group. They were very pleased. They had only been there a few months, but knew that they had the gifting and skills to do this. Having spent three years at theological college they felt that they had a wealth of knowledge to pass on to others and were glad their training minister had recognized this. They decided to put together five sessions on the subject they had enjoyed at college – Byzantine Iconoclasm. They thought it would be new to people. It would be easy to do as they could just cut and paste some of their old essays and could borrow some of the slides a friend had used for their presentation on the same subject. They wouldn't make things complicated by giving the friend the credit for the slides. They hoped by doing this they would be able to demonstrate their abilities and knowledge in a way that a mere sermon wouldn't. If anyone were to ask a difficult question they could answer it in such a way that it would be very unlikely anyone would ask another.

Skyler wanted to impress the congregation, particularly some of the more high-profile members. They decided to invite these higher-profile members personally, including the retired bishop. After some thought, they decided not to use the church with the instant tea and coffee and limp biscuits, but to meet at home and provide good quality coffee and cakes for the esteemed guests. (They would need to hide the TV and the DVDs and replace these with some impressive looking books.)

Skyler decided to borrow the large lectern from church. They could also record the lectures to upload on to YouTube – but would probably do this separately so they could get the sound right and make sure that they looked good on the screen. The evening was of course begun in prayer; an ancient piece of cleverly crafted prose that set the scene nicely for the lecture to come. Everyone listened carefully and although some looked slightly puzzled Skyler thought the evening was a great success They were very pleased with themselves.

Storm

Storm, a leader of a medium-sized church, decided that their congregation had become slack and had drifted from the truth. People had started to ask questions about their sermons and even worse, wonder aloud whether what was preached actually made sense in their everyday world. There was a definite need to explain (yet again!) the fundamental elements of the faith, and to reinforce the dire consequences of questioning them. As an aside this would also reinforce their own leadership and quell any notion that anyone else's voice should be heard, especially those who sowed doubt in other peoples' minds.

The following Sunday, Storm announced a Back to Basics course would be run, beginning that Wednesday evening from 7.30pm to 9.30pm. Many of the elderly didn't like coming out at night, and anyone with childcare responsibilities, or who were indeed children, would be unable to attend even if they wanted to. However, most of the men would be free to come, and they could explain everything to the others in their households. The stated intention was to bring people back in line with the one true faith, and the one true understanding of that faith. In fairness, Storm didn't really want to frighten people. It was just that they felt responsible for their proper belief and behaviour.

The evening began with prayer; extemporary and passionate, beginning with 'Oh Lord, we know that you are a God who is just like a slightly better version of us...'. There was a good attendance and everyone listened carefully; some even took notes. No one dared ask questions in case they looked silly or were thought a doubter. It was clear by the end that the leader had reasserted their alpha-status and order was restored. The evening ended on a high and everyone went to their various homes and asserted their own vicarious authority there. And for those who count silence as peace, there was peace on earth. Storm thought God would be pleased with them.

Each of the characters in the scenarios above had different motives, which revealed a different view of the participants, and led to a different approach to learning. Of course, these are caricatures and in real life we all have a mixture of motives and approaches. We hope what follows will be helpful to everyone, but it is specifically aimed at encouraging and equipping Sages.

1. Grown Up Learning in Church

The experience of teaching and learning we have had ourselves, especially as a child, will greatly influence our own approach. If we were unlucky, our experience may have been 'big teacher knows best and little children sit quietly, don't ask difficult questions and do learn by rote to repeat what is being taught'. This was the approach Skyler took.

Unfortunately, if we adopt the 'old school teacher' role in an adult learning group, and treat others like children, people tend to revert to 'old school mode'. It may appear to have the desired effect – everyone agrees with teacher – but in reality, everyone gets stuck in a bit of an unhealthy dynamic, with all sorts of bother bubbling under the surface, a lot of clock watching, and ultimately, learning for everyone involved eventually tends to be limited to knowing they don't want to do it again! This is because this approach fails to recognise the knowledge, experience, perspectives and practical wisdom of all those attending the session.

If we want people to grow in confidence and faith (and we do, don't we?) we need to take a different approach. Fortunately, good adult education theory helps us out. A lot of research has been done on how and why adults learn. What follows is an overview, which is not exhaustive, nor intended to be prescriptive. Everyone is different and no one fits neatly into any box.

The educationalist Malcom Knowles identified that adult learners are different to children in many ways.[1] Importantly, their learning is no

---

[1] Knowles, M. S., Holton III, E. F., Swanson, R. A., & Robinson, P. A. (2020). *The Adult Learner: the definitive classic in adult education and human resource development*. London: Routledge.

longer compulsory. They no longer have to go to school and instead are choosing to learn; something else is driving them. They have often moved from being dependent on others to being independent learners. They come to learning older and wiser, with a wealth of resources and experiences to draw on. This in turn can also mean they are more confident. They tend to prefer to learn about things that relate to life as it is lived and experienced. This is sometimes called problem-centred learning, as opposed to abstract learning for learning's sake. Often the learning desired is equipping for roles or responsibilities.

Take a moment to reflect on when you have taken a course or consciously learned something since you left school. Why did you do it? John Daines identifies the following reasons adults choose to learn:

- to follow up an existing interest
- to learn or develop ideas
- to create something
- to satisfy curiosity
- to save money
- to discover 'if I can'
- to gain the approval of others
- to obtain a qualification
- to access a further learning opportunity
- to meet like-minded people
- to make social contact
- to gain social confidence
- to enhance self-esteem[2]

We therefore aspire to a teaching theory called student-centred learning or learner-centred education.

---

[2] Daines, J., Daines, C., & Graham, B. (1993). *Adult Learning, Adult Teaching.* University of Nottingham.

It is helpful to remember that adults learn best when they:

- want to learn
- are involved in negotiating the content and delivery of learning
- diagnose their own needs
- derive their own goals
- are encouraged to be autonomous
- experience openness, trust, respect and commitment
- have responsibility for their own learning
- share ideas and feelings
- are in a climate conducive to learning
- are willing to alter their way of thinking
- are able to accept uncertainty
- learn and think with others
- make use of their experience
- are present-centred
- learn from problems rather than subjects
- are activity based
- focus on principles
- reflect on experience
- acknowledge the importance of process
- have a sense of progression
- are in an informal situation
- are equal partners in the learning process

All of this is important when thinking about the why, who, what and where of adult learning.

It also requires a very different approach to creating and delivering learning. Often, we use the term facilitation to describe this form of learning. We acknowledge the learner's desire to learn and the knowledge and experience each learner already has and explicitly seek to relate new knowledge with the old, allowing the learner to integrate the former with their existing learning. It seeks to meet learners where they are and let their learning grow from there.

This approach involves a reorientation of both mindsets and methods as outlined below.

Teacher-Centred Learning	Student-Centred Learning
Focus on teacher	Focus on learner
Knowledge is transmitted from teacher to learner	Learners construct their own knowledge
Teacher talks and learners listen passively	Learners and teachers all interact
Learner receives information	Learners are involved in information sharing
Learner works alone	Learners work in groups or pairs
There is no talking	There is lots of talking
The teacher supports learners	There is mutual support
Pre-determined learning	Negotiated learning
Teacher sticks to script	Learning adapts organically
Head-centred learning	Holistic learning
Teacher knows best	We are all pilgrims

Finally, unless you are keen on Skyler's approach, learning has to be open and accessible.

Some useful questions to ask might be:

- How will as many people as possible know about the learning event?

- Will they be able to get there?
- Will they feel secure?
- Will there be appropriate facilities?
- Will the learning be relevant to them?

- Have you thought about potential unconscious bias in teachers and learners?
- Who will not be around the table and why?
- How might we break down the barriers that make access difficult?
- Has consideration been given to how to help differently-abled folk attend and enjoy the learning?
- Has consideration been given to other learner needs, such as autism, dyslexia?

- Does the design or content of learning create barriers or discrimination against anyone?
- Have you been sensitive to stereotyping, and used inclusive and diverse resources?
- Will teaching methods be amenable to assistive technology?

- If not, would it help to use different platforms for learning or use different modes of presentation? Which ones?

It is important to remember that adults who want to learn more about their faith will come with additional motivations. Consider what these might be. These motivations can be very varied. They might want to learn more about why certain things happen in worship, to learn about prayer, to explore understandings of different laws and commandments, to get help with explaining their faith to others, to be resourced to tackle social justice issues. They might want to meet with other Christians to discuss and get different perspectives on how to be a Christian in a difficult work or family situation.

Each of the potential participants in faith learning will come with their own different motivations, experiences, preferences and personalities. This will mean groups may include those with different church traditions, attitudes, cultural preferences and experience, and ways of thinking about their faith.

Take a moment to think. What motives might people have when it comes to learning more about their faith? Which of these apply to you as a learner?

All this needs to be considered when thinking about potential participants and how best to facilitate learning. We now turn to think about this in some more detail.

Takeaways

- Adult learning is different to learning in childhood
- Adults have different motives in choosing to learn
- Adults bring a wealth of expertise, skills and experience
- Adult learning works best when it meets the adult learner where they are
- Adult learning needs to be accessible and inclusive

2. Learners

Learners come in all shapes and sizes. They may come joyfully; they may come reluctantly. They may come full of expectation; they may come full of trepidation. Don't underestimate how much fear people might be bringing, because of their experiences of learning in the past. Many remember experiences of shame, often relating to struggles with learning at school and the way teachers, fellow pupils and families have dealt with this. Some may struggle with aspects of learning such as reading. But remember too, that everyone brings something of value and has experience and knowledge to contribute to the learning process.

In his book *Honey from the Rock*, Rabbi Lawrence Kushner includes one of his own poems, 'Jigsaw'. The poem likens every lifetime to a jigsaw puzzle comprising many pieces which we spend our lives trying to assemble. None of us contains within ourselves all the pieces to our own puzzle, but everyone does carry, consciously or unconsciously, one or more pieces to another person's puzzle. We may never know when one of our own actions presents itself as a jigsaw piece which fits into another person's puzzle. The 'piece' may be worthless to us, but in presenting it to the person who needs that piece to assemble their own puzzle, we become a messenger of the Most High.[3]

As we start to think about how we lead Christian learning we need to begin with the learners we are working with. What are the demographics of those you are working with? How might this impact how you work with them? Here are some questions to prompt

---

[3] Kushner, L. (1977). *Honey from the Rock: Visions of Jewish Mystical Renewal.* New York: Harper and Row.

reflection on some of the issues that may be experienced in different scenarios:

- If you are young, what might the challenges be in leading a group with members who are the age of your parents or even grandparents?

- Does the group contain lots of people who are similar and one or two who are quite different? How might that feel for all concerned and what can you do to make sure everyone is heard and learns together?

- Are there any literacy issues in the group? What about specific learning needs which may impact people's capacity to take part?

- What is the role of prayer in your context? Do you pray from a book or choose your own words? Perhaps there are people who will happily pray out loud and others who would feel stressed if asked and prefer silence.

- Are there any learners with physical support needs?

Made in God's image

Our starting point for looking at a learner is that each one of us is made in the image of God (Genesis 1.27) and we are all unique, bringing different passions, skills, gifts and interests to the learning experience. This is expressed well in *The Message*'s version of 1 Corinthians 12.7:

> Each person is given something to do that shows who God is. Everyone gets in on it, everyone benefits. All kinds of things are handed out by the Spirit, and to all kinds of people! The variety is wonderful.

This verse is part of a passage where Paul talks about us together being the body of Christ and how we all have different parts to play in that. As we look to lead learning, one of the things we are trying to do is to help people find places where they can serve effectively and play their part in the mission and ministry of their local church or Christian organisation. We welcome and value diversity in our learning as that gives a richer learning experience as we learn from one another. As a leader of learning we often receive more than we give.

What impacts learning?

Think of something you do well. How did you get to being able to do this thing well?

Answering this question will give you an insight into learning. Everyone we work with will have had some experience of successful learning for us to build on. Generally speaking, learning with adults is most likely to be successful when the following elements are in place:

- Wanting to learn – freely choosing to join the learning process, and able to help shape it

- Needing to learn for all sorts of reasons (and it is down to us sometimes to help people see what the need is)

- Learning through doing – practicing, using trial and error, building time in for this

- Processing, reflecting and making sense of learning – often needs time and facilitation

- Improving through feedback – how do you know how you are doing if no one feeds back?

A helpful way of visualising this is to imagine throwing a pebble into a pond and seeing the ripples spread out. If we can motivate people to understand why they want or need to do the training, then that spreads out to having a go, processing the learning and then hopefully seeking feedback to continue to develop. There are a lot of ministry contexts where this may be a helpful process.

In what way might you build the factors in the bullet points above into what you do?

More things to think about

There are eight further elements we may want to think about in relation to our learners and all of them can impact how they learn and their experiences of learning with us:

- **Cultural** – we arrive at a learning opportunity with years of messages about learning and ourselves as a learner. These can be positive, but sadly, they are often negative. In the church this culture can sometimes be interpreted as "that's not for people like me"!

- **Emotional** – how we feel at any given time can have a big influence on how we participate in something and how we perceive it. Again, for some, learning might trigger negative emotions from wrong messages received as a child. Or, if something significant has happened that day (good or bad) those emotions may overshadow our ability to learn.

- **Environmental** – how long can you sit on an uncomfortable chair for? At what temperature do you begin to get sleepy or conversely feel so cold you can't concentrate? Sound and light can affect people too. The physical environment makes a big difference in terms of how easily a learner may be able to access and enjoy the learning.

- **Physiological** – similarly, our internal physical condition also affects our learning. If we are thinking about drink, food or when the next toilet break will be it may well disrupt our learning. Let people know when breaks will be and reduce anxiety by anticipating mobility issues.

- **Psychological** – we all differ in how we see the world, and we don't all realise that others see things differently. Take time to understand the existing frameworks of thinking and stories of understanding which people are bringing with them.

- **Personality** – we also all have different personalities and will see and engage with things differently because of that.

- **Sociological** – it is not just our educational backgrounds but also our wider social, economic and geographical differences we bring to learning. These can quite dramatically affect group dynamics.

- **Spiritual** – our approach to spirituality will impact our meaning-making, connectedness and sense of purpose. Religious dimensions, such as how we see God, our self and our vocation, may impact how we arrive at a learning event.

Some of these you cannot influence, but being aware of them can help you understand your learners a little better. These factors may also help you to think ahead about how your leadership of learning might need to be adjusted to accommodate everyone.

Multiple intelligences

Another of the ways we can appreciate the diversity of each other is through Howard Gardner's theory of multiple intelligences. We are including multiple intelligences to encourage you to think about the different strengths people may bring, and to encourage you to see intelligence in different ways. Gardner suggests we all have different strengths and that we should celebrate the breadth of intelligences that we have.[4] Gardner proposes eight different intelligences.

	Intelligence	Description	Example
Word smart	Linguistic	good at understanding and using the spoken and written word	Oprah Winfrey
Number smart	Logical / mathematical	good with numbers and at problem solving	Bill Gates
Picture smart	Spatial	good at working in three dimensions and strong visual memory	Amelia Earhart
Body smart	Bodily / kinaesthetic	good at using the body to help learn and remember	Lionel Messi
Music smart	Musical	good with pitch, rhythm and melodies	Adele
People smart	Intrapersonal	good self-understanding and sense of identity	Mother Teresa
Self smart	Interpersonal	good communication skills verbal and non-verbal, empathetic	Maya Angelou
Nature smart	Naturalist	good at reading and understanding their environment	David Atten-borough

---

[4] Gardner, H. E. (2000). *Intelligence Reframed: multiple intelligences for the 21st century*. Hachette UK. Explore multiple intelligences further at: https://www.literacynet.org/mi/assessment/findyourstrengths.html. This is a version you can print out and use with others: https://www.businessballs.com/freepdfmaterials/free_multiple_intelligences_test_manual_version.pdf.

Noticing and affirming people for their different strengths is important as it demonstrates we value a range of different skills and gifts, including our own. It can also be a fun challenge to try to include elements of learning that give everyone a chance to use the intelligence they are most gifted in by ensuring that our content is varied and bears this understanding in mind. This will also then include different preferences, as we explore in the next section.

Takeaways

- We all learn in different ways and have strengths in a variety of areas
- Each learner comes with their unique experiences, which may both hinder and help them
- Seek to help people identify their particular strengths and preferences
- Affirm and appreciate diversity
- Consider how learning can be holistic

3. How People Learn

There are many different theories that can help us understand more about how people learn. We are going to explore some of them in this section. We hope they are helpful in identifying some of your own preferences in the way you learn, and also in putting together learning for others, which helps those with different preferences to engage.

Global and analytic learning

With this theory, the two ways people approach learning might be summed up as the difference between those of us who will always study the jigsaw box lid or read the instructions for putting together some module furniture from beginning to end before we start, and those of us who just plunge in! As with all of these types of lists, we don't necessarily fit neatly into one to the exclusion of the other.

Global learning	Analytic learning
Focuses on the big picture – sees the wood	Emphasizes details – sees the trees
May work better in groups	May work better alone
Tends to make decisions based on intuition or emotion	Tends to make decisions based on logic, facts, common sense
Enjoys doing several things at once	Enjoys doing one thing at a time
Processes information randomly or sees patterns	Processes information sequentially

Global learning	Analytic learning
Can work with distractions and likes frequent breaks	Likes to work in an organized and structured environment

Clearly it is difficult to accommodate all these things as some of them are very different to each other, but we may want to think about how we might draw on this theory in our learning planning.

You can do an online test to help you work out which you are: http://www.whatismylearningstyle.com/global-vs-analytic-test.html.

What follows is a brief introduction to some of the other main learning theories, with information on how to explore them in more detail.

VARK

VARK was developed into an inventory by Neil Fleming from New Zealand in 1987.[5] He suggests that there are four learning preferences:

- **Visual** – learning through seeing

- **Auditory** – learning through listening

- **Read/Write** – learning through reading and writing

- **Kinaesthetic** – learning through doing something physical

---

[5] Fleming, N. D. (1995, July). I'm different; not dumb. Modes of presentation (VARK) in the tertiary classroom. In *Research and development in higher education, Proceedings of the 1995 Annual Conference of the Higher Education and Research Development Society of Australasia (HERDSA)*, HERDSA (Vol. 18, pp. 308-313). You can take a test to see what you come out as here: https://vark-learn.com/. There is also lots of information on this site as to how to incorporate these different preferences into your teaching and learning.

The advantage of this model is that it is very easy to understand and explain to others.

Kolb's Learning Cycle

This is also sometimes called Kolb's reflective cycle.[6] A number of learning theories are based upon it and so it is worth taking the time to understand it. Basically, David Kolb suggests that as an individual learns they move through a series of stages: that is, they experience, reflect, conceptualise and then apply. He identifies that learning begins when people have an experience or learn something new. They then reflect on it and decide how to make it fit into their existing knowledge. Finally, they decide how they will adapt their behaviour based upon their new understanding. The theory is often represented in the form of a diagram like the one below.

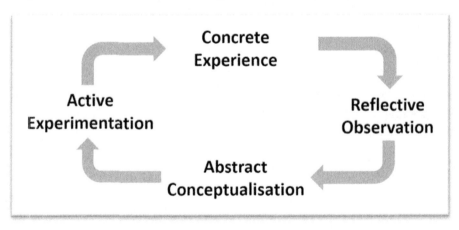

Concrete
Experience

Reflective
Observation

Active
Experimentation

Abstract
Conceptualisation

---

[6] Kolb, D. A. (2007). *The Kolb Learning Style Inventory*. Boston, MA: Hay Resources Direct.
You can learn more here: https://www.simplypsychology.org/learning-kolb.html.

4MAT

One model based on the work of Kolb has been developed by Bernice McCarthy.[7] She suggests there are four learning styles, which are detailed in the table below.

Learning style	Description	Key question
Imaginative	Like the big picture; learn by listening and sharing ideas; learn best with others; can see different sides of issue.	Why do I want to learn this? Meaning
Analytic	Learn by watching and listening; like being teacher led; want all the information before making a decision; like facts; critique information.	What do I want to learn? Content
Common sense	Enjoy playing with ideas to see if they work in real life; enjoy analysing and solving real world problems; learn by doing; pragmatic.	How does this work? Experiment
Dynamic	Like following hunches or intuition and seeing where they end up; flexible; enjoy change; value originality.	What could this become? Creative application

Thinking about how you answer all four of those questions in any session can be a useful way of checking that you are covering all the learning styles that help people learn best.

---

[7] McCarthy, B., & McCarthy, D. (2006). *Teaching around the 4MAT® cycle: Designing instruction for diverse learners with diverse learning styles*. Thousand Oaks, CA: Corwin Press.

Honey and Mumford

Honey and Mumford also follow Kolb's learning cycle.[8] They identify four different learning styles.

Learning style	Description
Activist	Involve themselves in new experiences and thrive on activity. Open-minded and happy to tackle problems head-on.
Theorist	Adapt and integrate experiences and learning into logical theories. Detached, analytical and happy to think deeply about problems.
Pragmatist	Down to earth and focussed on problem solving. Practically minded and happy to try out ideas to see if they work.
Reflector	Stand back and ponder ideas from different perspectives. Thoughtful, cautious and happy to collect lots of data.

Developmental relationships

If we are going to be involved with people long term, then it can be helpful to think about what sort of relationship we want to develop with them. The following framework from the Search Institute was originally written for work with young people.[9] We have adapted it slightly for wider learning groups. The Aims are what we as facilitators of learning might seek to do within a relationship, and the

---

[8] Honey, P., & Mumford, A. (1989). *Learning Styles Questionnaire*. Organization Design and Development, Incorporated.

[9] You can find out more here: https://www.search-institute.org/developmental-relationships/developmental-relationships-framework/.

Actions are suggestions as to how we might achieve it from the learner's perspective.

Aims	Actions
Express Care	Be dependable – be someone I can trust Listen – be present to me Believe in me – make me feel known and valued Be warm – show me you enjoy being with me Encourage – praise me
Challenge Growth	Expect my best – live up to my potential Stretch – encourage me to go further Hold me accountable – responsible for my own actions Reflect – help me to learn from experience
Provide Support	Empower – build my confidence Set boundaries – keep me on track
Share Power	Respect me – treat me fairly and with dignity Collaborate – work with me in solving problems Let me lead – create opportunities for me to lead
Expand possibilities	Inspire – help me to see new possibilities for the future Broaden horizons – expose me to new ideas, experiences Connect – introduce me to people who can help me grow

Takeaways

- Think of introductory activities or content which incorporates both global and analytic preferences
- Remember that participants may enjoy learning in different ways, so include a variety of modes of learning

- Consider talking about learning preferences with participants to help them understand how they learn
- Understand your own preferred ways of learning and ensure you don't just use them!
- For each participant consider what dimension of developmental relationships may be most appropriate for them

4. Learning Spaces

Teaching and learning in the church takes place in many way and contexts, and in many different sorts of spaces. Depending on the ministry you are involved in and where you are, one or more of the spaces below may resonate with you.

A PARENTING COURSE:
One of the churches in a small market town runs a regular parenting course during the day, which it offers to parents or people in parenting roles at the local school. The meetings take place in the school community room for eight afternoons in the spring term. The material for the course was developed by members of the church team with expertise in this area. They have then trained others to help deliver this course.

A CHURCHES TOGETHER LENT COURSE:
Churches Together in a rural community run an annual Lent course. People from different churches in the community are asked to host and lead a group using the study material that has been decided upon for that year. Meetings take place once a week over Lent.

EXTERNAL SPEAKERS:
An urban church has a monthly meeting on a Friday evening where a 'high-profile' Christian guest speaker is asked to give a talk on an area of their expertise in a large community hall. Topics covered have included: the environment, the book of Revelation and the goodness of God.

ZOOM SEMINAR:
A lay minister is leading a series of seminars looking at the lives of women of the Bible. The group of women attending already meet

regularly twice a month in order to pray, share and learn. The group is geographically distant but able to meet online.

BAPTISM PREPARATION:
A significant number of families in the area surrounding a suburban church, which has an active children's ministry, ask for their children to be baptised. A small team of people from the church are involved in baptism preparation, including visiting the family at home and welcoming them to a series of baptism classes taking place on a Sunday morning after the church service.

MENTORING:
A large church with a number of young interns on a national programme has set up a mentoring scheme. In this scheme, a more experienced church member is asked to meet with an intern on a one-to-one basis in the church prayer room, twice each month.

REFLECTIVE GROUPS:
The regional church has a reflective group scheme for those training for lay and ordained ministry. Each group of eight people, meets at the main church office once a month for three hours to reflect on life and ministry together. A trained person facilitates the discussions.

Spaces in teaching and learning

Teaching and learning in its varied types and sizes takes place in many 'spaces': virtually, in homes, in church, in church halls, in gardens or in community buildings. This space may need to accommodate large groups, small groups, families, or those who meet on a one-to-one basis. It may also need to be able to host anything from a one-off meeting, to a series of meetings over a number of years. Whatever may be happening in it, there are some important things to remember.

1. Prayed-into spaces

Whatever the context, praying into the space in which we are meeting both blesses it, and helps prepare ourselves to lead the learning. This may include praying for the session before it even happens, as we arrive into the space, be that a Zoom room or a physical room, and before the meeting begins. Each time we pray it is a reminder that we are standing on holy ground, and that God is present and will reveal himself as he sees fit. When everyone is gone, it is also good to give thanks in that place and in that space.

2. Practical spaces

Different types of learning events are enabled by different environments. A group meeting once a week to share what has been happening in their lives and to share what God has been doing is probably better placed in a home environment with chairs in the living room or around a dining room table, rather than meeting and sitting on pews in church. A meeting for mums with toddlers will need space and toys and an accessible toilet with a child seat. Finding the best available, affordable and accessible venue is worth the time and effort.

3. Accessible spaces

Accessibility is key. For those who are differently-abled, the lack of a lift, or a hearing loop, or a large text programme may limit involvement or even prevent attendance. For those who are less confident, arriving at a meeting with someone else can make possible what would be very difficult alone. During the pandemic, many previously reluctant people were introduced to digital equipment and services and began using online teaching resources. This has made 'attendance' for those who are housebound more feasible. For those less technically confident or with variable internet connectivity, a backup phone number in case of problems can be of great help. Accessibility also relates to timing. It is good to ensure that those who are absent at one meeting have a say in deciding when and where the next meeting should be.

4. Welcoming spaces

Welcome is more than greeting someone on arrival; it is about having a welcoming heart. It is sometimes helpful to think about how Jesus welcomes us and to ask him for the grace to be truly hospitable to others. Perhaps people may even feel the welcome of Jesus through us. It helps to welcome with eyes as well as voices, and treat everyone as an honoured guest. On a Zoom screen this can be about looking at each face on the screen for a few extra seconds and quietly speaking a prayer of welcome into the space. Or, it can be about looking around the room and, whether you catch the eyes of the person or not, breathing a prayer of welcome.

5. Hospitable spaces

Welcome is part of hospitality, the act of service by which we receive and host those in attendance. Jesus and food seem to be a wonderful model here: might you offer coffee, tea, cake, or even meals? Hospitality also means caring about the details. This may involve providing additional refreshment that does not have gluten or meat or sugar. Or it may be about not having particular refreshments for the health and wellbeing of others, such as peanuts or alcohol. It may also be about signposting the toilets or where coats can be stored safely.

6. Respectful spaces

Respectful spaces see each person as the unique child of God that they are. There are no celebrities in a family. The space is a space of mutuality, where leaders expect to learn as much, if not more, than they impart. It is a space that enables all to be fully present, to realise more deeply who they are, and especially who they are in God.

Depending on the context, for example in reflective or sharing groups, this may include agreeing group rules concerning confidentiality. In other contexts, it might be about noticing when the behaviour of one group member is disrespectful of another and discerning how to deal with it.

7. Safe spaces

Safe spaces are places where safeguarding has been considered as a priority from the outset, rather than as an afterthought. DBS checks and safeguarding training need to have been done well in advance and learning needs to be embedded in that practice. Guidance and structures for how to respond to any safeguarding events, need to be clear and transparent. Risk assessments need to be carried out carefully and prayerfully, not just as a 'formality'.

But safe spaces are about more than these safeguarding necessities. Safe spaces have agreed levels of confidentiality. They are places where power dynamics have been considered wisely; preferably where the person leading is accountable and ideally in supervision for their role. Safe spaces are those where attention is given to who might be able to over-hear, particularly in the summer when doors and windows may be open or if the meeting takes place in a garden.

Consideration is also needed to ensure the space is safe for the person leading. This may be about ensuring that one-to-one meetings take place with others around or where a glass door allows what is happening behind it to be seen whilst not being heard. In home visiting, it is about letting someone else know your diary, where you will be and when you expect to be finished. Risk assessments are often readily available for a venue, but as a leader you will also need to do a risk assessment for the learning event itself.

Take a few minutes to think about your own context. Use the table below to help you plan how you might consider, create and curate the spaces for the following hypothetical learning events in your own church of community.

- A PARENTING COURSE
- A CHURCHES TOGETHER LENT COURSE
- A SERIES OF EXTERNAL SPEAKERS
- AN ONLINE SEMINAR
- BAPTISM PREPARATION
- MENTORING
- REFLECTIVE GROUPS

Consider the space in the light of the people

1. The people who will be there as learners.
2. The people who will be leading, helping and facilitating.
3. The seven dimensions of spaces before and after:
    prayed into; welcoming; practical; accessible; hospitable; respectful; safe.

Create the space in the light of the venue

1. Equipment, refreshments, technology.
2. Risk assessments and safety.
3. Accessibility, comfort, welcome, hospitality.

Curate the space in the light of the learning process

1. The material to be covered.
2. How the material will be covered and the room will be used.
3. How God will be acknowledged, invited and involved.

Now spend some time looking at the learning events that are happening in your church and community. What might you do to make the space more prayed in, practical, accessible, welcoming, hospitable, respectful and safe?

Takeaways

- Physical environment needs to be appropriate for the learning
- Provide a hospitable space – physically and spiritually
- Consider practicalities in advance: power sockets; IT requirements; refreshment facilities; opening and closing the venue
- Think about preventing harm; remember risk assessments and safeguarding
- Pray and prepare and pray again

5. Learning Content

The previous chapters have demonstrated that there are all sorts of things that need to be taken into account when considering leading learning. This chapter moves on to ask similar questions about selecting the sort of content and activities offered in a learning session.

If you have got the inclination to put together some learning from scratch then go for it; it is great fun. However, not everyone has the time or talent (and even if they have both, the confidence) to do that, at least to begin with. It is fortunate therefore that there are plenty of courses around that can just be picked up off the shelf. These can be used just as they are, or taken as a start point for you to adapt to your particular context. In any case, it is good to follow the same thought processes and make sure that they are chosen, adapted or created to suit what and how your particular group want to learn.

It is always wise to first of all spend time and prayer thinking about what you feel called to offer, to listen to prospective learners to find out what they want and need, and then to find some common ground. Having agreed a topic, it is time to think through how to choose the content.

Questions to ask:

- What are the overall aims? Is the overall purpose to: increase knowledge; deepen understanding; change attitudes, beliefs or behaviours; impart information; stimulate action; or something else?

- What are the specific objectives? What might be achievable stepping stones that lead towards the aims? What will the learner be able to identify, demonstrate, show, etc. at the end of a successful session?

- How much time can I give to preparation? (Be fair to yourself and your other commitments!)

- What skills do I / the group have / not have? Doing a skills audit as a group is a great icebreaker and gives people confidence in what they are bringing to the table.

- What are the limitations imposed by the place we will be meeting in? Or the technology available?

The type of method you might choose will depend on the objective. For example, if the objective is to teach a physical skill, then demonstration, discovery method, individual practice and just having a go will be helpful. If the objective is to impart knowledge, then talks, suggested private study and reading and tutorials will work well. If the objective is to change attitudes, then using case studies, group discussions or perhaps devising and executing a local project will make the learning human and 'real'.

A note of caution. You will have your own preferences based on your skill-set, experience and simply what you enjoy. However, please do remember that not everyone is the same and try to include a range of different content and learning styles to engage all those attending.

Four main methods

There are four main methods we use in teaching and training, and the activities we choose will usually fit into one of these.

- **Presentation** – this is up front, teacher / trainer-led and includes such things as demonstrations, PowerPoints and related software such as Prezi, what is sometimes called old-fashioned chalk and talk, handouts, flipcharts, whiteboards, etc.

- **Participatory** – this involves interaction between the teacher / trainer and learner and will include such things as question and answer sessions, class discussions, breakout groups, post-it note activities, etc.

- **Discovery or experiential** – this involves learners working on their own or in groups on different tasks or activities, which can include reading and writing as well as practice, role plays, creating, art, etc.

- **Evaluatory** – we also need to evaluate the learning we are doing, so things like quizzes, simulation exercises and tests may be appropriate. Activities like these can act not only as an evaluation of what has gone before, but also a 'check-in' to find out whether we are on track for the future in terms of expectations, involvement and learning.

As you choose your different methods, bear in mind things which can impact what methods and activities you choose and how successful they are:

- The make-up of the group you are working with – including any specific needs you are aware of

- Where you are delivering your teaching or training – is it online or face to face; what is the size of venue and what resources are available?

- The team delivering the training or teaching – what do they feel comfortable doing, what skills or expertise do they bring?

- Ask yourself whether you are uncomfortable with an activity – will those you are working with pick up on your feelings?

- The topic you are covering – fun activities might not always be appropriate, for example when discussing ethical issues or pastoral care

- The individual learners and their learning preferences

The important thing is to be prayerfully brave and include different activities in facilitating learning. This demonstrates that you are learning too. It also teaches that diversity is not just acceptable, but good fun!

The two tables below give examples of how different content is received by different learning preferences based on two of the theories discussed in Chapter 3.

VARK	Enjoy	Don't enjoy
Visual Learners	Snappy presentations, videos, using imagination, pictures, graphics, doodling, flow charts	messy work space, cluttered presentations
Auditory Learners	traditional lecturing and discussions, panels and debates, listening to podcasts, pair and group work, music and presentations	sitting still for too long, going too fast, few opportunities for participation
Read / Write Learners	text-based information, reading themselves, well organised text with sub-headings and text books	someone reading to them, distractions

VARK	Enjoy	Don't enjoy
Kinaesthetic Learners	demonstrations, 'hands-on' experience, experiments, exercises, role plays, presentation of processes and drama	things going too slow, poor use of colour, few opportunities for practical application of ideas

Honey & Mumford	Enjoy	Don't enjoy
Activists	role play, simulation games, competitive team games, drama, sculpting, workshops, brain-storming, projects, visits	being passive observers, dealing with lots of data, too much theory, working on their own, repetition
Theorists	lectures, guided reading, programmed learning, tutorials, supervision, note taking, seminars, analysis, critical thinking	not knowing the bigger picture, lack of structure, emphasis on feelings, lack of depth, ambiguity in instructions
Reflectors	good briefing, discussions, debates, panels of experts, doing research, time to consider, opportunities for listening, distance learning	action without planning, overly constraining instructions, insufficient data for a conclusion, being rushed
Pragmatists	case studies, demonstrations, on the job learning, meeting the expert, workshops, training seminars, agenda setting, problem solving	learning not related to need, no practice involved, going round in circles, obstacles to putting learning into practice

Takeaways

- Is the content relevant and interesting to the learners?
- Will the learning make a practical or significant difference?
- Have I considered the motivations for learning?
- Have I thought about different learning preferences?
- Have I included material that people with different gifts can contribute to?

6. Jesus: The Creative Teacher

Don't worry if you sit down to plan a session and your mind is blank. Just ask 'what would Jesus do?'! Jesus used many different ways of teaching or facilitating learning. In this chapter, we explore ten of them with examples of how we might use them in our context. Some of the ideas fit under multiple headings. They largely come without detailed explanations as we want to invite you to imagine how they might be used in your context and in ways which will work for your group. Use them to spark your own creativity!

Storytelling – parables like the Good Shepherd and their sheep (John 10.1-21)

Share your favourite story from childhood and explain how it has influenced you.

Ask people to create a book cover, or game, song or movie poster with a title on it that reflects their story or the story you are studying.

Compose and perform an action song.

Reframe a story – for example what would the Palm Sunday story look like in contemporary London?

Watch and discuss a video – anything from a short clip on YouTube to a full-length film.

Ask individuals to write or create their own stories using whatever medium they like best.

Ask the group to create a collaborative or individual picture, mural or frieze to illustrate a story.

Write a summary of the story in no more characters than a tweet (280).

Use social media like Tik-Tok, Snap or another platform to create a summary of a story.

Use a guided meditation or reflection to help people enter into the story. Tell the story slowly and ask people to imagine themselves as part of the scene, with the option to share what they experienced. Perhaps ask people to take up a character in a Bible or other story and then stop at a certain point and ask them to continue with the story themselves or answer a question asked.

Using metaphors – like I am the light of the world or the bread of life in John's Gospel (John 6.35)

Invite people to play with clay, play dough, or crayons to illustrate their response to a particular image or issue.

Ask people what metaphors they might use to illustrate a particular situation or experience.

Create a list of metaphors for God and ask people to choose their most and least liked, and explain why.

Create an Instagram picture for a particular metaphor.

Teachable moments – like the Woman at the Well (John 4.5-26)

Sometimes the time is just right for learning. To try to prompt this you might want to use an icebreaker – an introductory activity to begin the learning. This can be an activity or something you present to start the session. Some people use experience bingo with a new group – you make up relevant categories and you go around the room collecting signatures on the card. Keep it fun, for example, have a birthday in February, only child, washed their hair today or have a pet.

Make a poster in response to a local community issue or topical concern that has created a teachable moment for the group.

Draw a comic strip of the teachable moment.

Host debates with individuals or groups presenting each side, e.g. "Does the Bible support being vegetarian?"

Have a box where people can put their questions and periodically answer them.

Ask individuals or the group to create a social media status update for a particular person, situation, etc.

Developing self-awareness and identity – like Peter's discipleship (Matthew 16.18)

Choose a song which you think reflects your personality or an aspect of yourself, for example, which song would you like to be played as you collect an award?

Ask people to devise a coat of arms which reflects their personality and different aspects of their life.

Use one of the sets of pictures of Jesus or gather some and ask people to choose the one which is closest to their own picture of Jesus and encourage the group to explore their choices.

Create timelines, for example the ups and downs of my Christian journey.

Ask people to bring something which illustrates the topic and host a 'show and tell' for the group.

Create mind maps based on core beliefs or how faith impacts your daily life.

You can find lots of self-assessment exercises online, ranging from which disciple you resemble (https://churchleaders.com/daily-buzz/248447-which-disciple-are-you-take-short-quiz-find.html) to what your preferred leadership style may be (https://www.businessballs.com/leadership-models/leadership-styles-quiz/). You can ask people to complete this beforehand or, in some settings, they can do this on their phone in the session and share.

Pip Wilson's blob trees (https://www.blobtree.com/) can be used in lots of different ways but particularly asking where people are, where they would like to be and how they think they can get there.

Problem solving – like the Rich Young Ruler (Mark 10.17-22)

Use ranking exercises in relation to different solutions to a problem, for example what are the top three community outreach activities we could do next term.

Devise word games, such as crosswords, hangman etc., with all the key concepts you want to explore in them.

Identify a problem and list as many ways as possible of solving it; or ask key questions such as what, where, why, how, who, when, etc.

Focus on a case study and draw out what can be learnt from it for your particular situation.

Create an individual or group mind map to explore a problem or an issue.

Write a letter to an agony aunt or give the group a letter which they have to respond to.

Lecture or talk – like the Sermon on the Mount (Matthew 5-7)

Create a series of PowerPoint slides or similar for a talk or lecture.

Write or perform a monologue from a particular perspective, for example Mary after the visit of the angel to tell her she would become pregnant or Noah when God told him to build an ark.

Ask the group to do a presentation about a particular story, learning point, illustration, etc.

Create a handout or worksheet to go alongside a lecture or a talk.

Record a sermon and then watch and critique it with the group.

Illustrations – for example from nature (Matthew 6.26-34)

Make up an acrostic, i.e., find a word for each of the letters of the key point of the illustration or object lesson, for example TRUST – Trustworthy, Reliable, Understanding, Supportive, Together.

Make a collage to reflect a key point or saying, for example Do not be afraid / Fear not.

Use poetry or creative writing to share an insight.

Use art as a starting point for reflection, for example, ask everyone for a one-minute reflection on an aspect of discipleship based on a picture or photograph.

Provide some art materials for people to create their own illustration.

Identify what you want to explore and then send people off on a 'scavenger hunt' to get items to contribute. This can work for online or outdoor events. For example, items might be something that is growing, something small or something bright.

Asking questions – like what good is the whole world if the soul is lost? (Matthew 16.26)

Use 'on the line activities', for example, ask people to position themselves in a line (where one end is very comfortable and the other very uncomfortable) in answer to a question such as "How comfortable are you with inviting a friend to church?" You could also use sides of the room or corners and have several options to respond. You can then ask people to explain why they have chosen where they are.

Create a feedback or other form where people have to indicate how they feel by emoji.

Write a letter to answer one of the questions Jesus asks, for example "Do you love me?" in John 21.16-17. (The more personal the question, the more you may want to keep the responses private with optional sharing.)

Invite a panel that people can pose questions to on the topic of the session.

Card sorting exercises can be used to answer questions, like "What are the three top priorities for the church in the year ahead?" or "What are the top five qualities of a leader?" (You will need to have prepared sets of cards in advance for people to put in order of preference.)

Creating experiences – like the sending out of the twelve (Luke 9.1-10)

Outdoor activities are great for creating experiences for participants to reflect on, for example an awareness walk where you ask people to go for a walk on their own or with others looking for signs of God and to bring back (if appropriate) something that has spoken to them.

Set a simulation exercise. You could make your own but lots of voluntary sector organizations have examples you could use. The following link provides a good example from Christian Aid: https://www.christianaid.org.uk/sites/default/files/2017-08/disaster-zone-secondary-simulation-game.pdf.

Choose an experience you want your group to learn from, for example foot washing in a session on leadership.

Do a Treasure Hunt, Trail etc. with reflection questions: https://www.muddychurch.co.uk/ has some great examples.

Conversation – like 'Who then can be saved?' (Mark 10.26-29)

Role play a biblical or historical character to understand a particular issue, for example, interview Peter after he betrayed Jesus but before the crucifixion or Esther after her actions had saved her people.

Invite people to discuss an issue from two different perspectives, for example, Mary and Martha and the visit of Jesus to their house in Luke 10.38-42.

Use collections of postcards as conversation starters, for example, ask people to choose one that reflects how they are feeling and share in pairs or with the group.

Takeaways

- Work out which teaching methods are best for what you want to achieve in your session
- Variety is the spice of life – use different activities over a period of time for groups which meet regularly
- Look at the different ways Jesus taught and come up with your own ideas drawing upon his example
- Reflect on whether you have chosen the best method and activities for what you are wanting to teach
- Have you worked out how to evaluate your session? Form, discussion, activity?

7. Learning and Mission

The aim of this chapter is to explore examples of learning in different missional contexts. We will explore teaching and learning skills within: the church context; relational learning; small group learning; accessing and using resources and people; giving a talk or lecture. Each of the examples will be mapped against a mark of mission.

After each example you are invited to consider the following questions:

- How do you react to the example?
- What draws you in and what are you resistant to, and why do you think this might be?
- Where have you seen or been involved in similar missional learning in the past?
- What possibilities do you see in your context?
- What skills do you and those you minister with already have or could develop?
- Is there anyone else you could invite to be involved?

Do note your responses to these questions as it is often in noticing our heart-felt reactions to learning that we can discern where God is calling us. Often, as we are called to learn and develop new skills and abilities, our growth zone is just outside our comfort zone, but where God calls God equips!

Mission and vocation are intertwined. As Frederick Buechner said, 'Vocation is the place where our deep gladness meets the world's deep need.'[10] As you read the following scenarios, you may have

---

[10] Buechner, F. (1993). *Wishful Thinking: a seeker's ABC*. San Francisco, CA: HarperSanFrancisco, p. 144.

different reactions. Maybe you feel more comfortable about the idea of giving a talk than running a small group. Maybe the idea of leading a Grave Talk session is a challenge, as you normally prefer to be helping in the background and not at the front, but the idea of meeting with two or three people over coffee once a week to share faith journeys and discuss scripture excites you. Maybe you don't have a church nursery but do have a Carers' and Toddlers Group. Maybe you have poor links with school, but good ones with Girls' and Boys' Brigade. Hopefully, this chapter will get you thinking about your own context. Many people love to learn, and having learning opportunities provided can be a gift and blessing to those seeking them. They are also an intrinsic part of the mission of the church.

Marks of mission

Most churches have implicit or explicit mission statements. The Church of England, for example, has what it calls the five marks of mission. These are to help crystallise what mission is about. The five marks are:

- To proclaim the Good News of the Kingdom
- To teach, baptise and nurture new believers
- To respond to human need by loving service
- To seek to transform unjust structures of society and challenge violence of every kind and to pursue peace and reconciliation
- To strive to safeguard the integrity of creation and sustain and renew the life of the earth

These five marks are sometimes abbreviated to the five words: TELL – TEACH – TEND – TRANSFORM – TREASURE. You might find it helpful to see what sounds, images or passages of scripture come to mind when you read these words in the context of learning. The places we are in and the people we are with are all different, and as a result missional learning is going to vary.

Proclaiming the Good News of the Kingdom

While we may have natural skills in teaching and learning, we often need to learn from others before we are able to teach others. Consider this situation:

Members of the suburban church you belong to have raised the possibility of developing a team to offer to pray with people on the street outside the local shops. They have contacted another church in a similar area that has a well-established programme and training for those who want to take part. This church has offered to come and help lead a series of training workshops and to support your church in the first year. They have advised about necessary safeguarding and DBS requirements. They have also indicated that it would be helpful for a couple of the members of your church to train with them as trainers so that new people can be added to your team as time goes on. You have no prior experience of teaching in the church but have done some training of others as a result of your work in retail. You are wondering if you are being called to bring some of these skills into your role in the church and you are feeling very drawn to this missional ministry.

This example is about developing the skills and abilities of people to enable learning in the church. It demonstrates how reinventing the wheel may not be the best way forward, and accessing the skills and experience and expertise of others may well be a helpful way forward. The fact that some members of the church will be trained as trainers is one way of ensuring sustainability.

- How do you react to the example?
- What draws you in and what are you resistant to, and why do you think this might be?
- Where have you seen or been involved in similar missional learning in the past?
- What possibilities do you see in your context?

- What skills do you and those you minister with already have or could develop?
- Is there anyone else you could invite to be involved?

Where are the opportunities for your church to learn from others? This learning may be from a church or organization close by, or further afield. In either case it is also building relationship and trust across the kingdom.

Nurturing new believers

Learning does not have to be structured and formal. It can take place as people meet together and share over coffee. Consider this situation:

The church has developed small 'faith bubble groups' as a follow on from a discipleship course. The idea is that two or three people from the course meet once a week at the local coffee shop with a more established church member to share their journey of faith and pray with each other. Each week a different passage of scripture is chosen to be read, shared and discussed. You have been asked to be one of the more established church members willing to take on this coordinating and facilitating role. While nurturing growth in others is something that has always been part of who you are, you feel a bit unprepared for this.

As we listen to the stories others tell of what God has been doing in their lives we learn about them, about God and about the world. As we share scripture together, we learn to consider the word of God in the context of our lived experience. The layout of the coffee shop and price of coffee and who pays are important considerations that impact on confidentiality and accessibility. However, this learning is low key and these informal places offer significant opportunities for nurture, informal mentoring and peer support.

- How do you react to the example?
- What draws you in and what are you resistant to, and why do you think this might be?
- Where have you seen or been involved in similar missional learning in the past?
- What possibilities do you see in your context?
- What skills do you and those you minister with already have or could develop?
- Is there anyone else you could invite to be involved?

New believers are often hungry for more information and chances to share their growing faith with others. Asking new believers what they want to learn about and how they would like to learn about it helps enable self-directed approaches to ongoing growth and learning in faith. Many of these learning opportunities can also be made available to the wider community who may not have had the chance to ask the questions that they want or to learn about specific aspects of their faith. Of course, nurturing new believers can also be more formal and there are a number of established discipleship programmes available.

Responding to human need by loving service

End-of-life issues are difficult but necessary topics of conversation. Issues may include the illness or death of a family member or friend, health care, problems with social care, the need for sheltered housing or organising legal documents such as power of attorney for health and finance. These concerns can become significant and cause anxiety.

Grave Talk is a resource that has been prepared to help people talk about end-of-life issues. It comprises 50 cards which each have a question to get the conversation started.[11] They come with a guide for the facilitator and guidance on running an event. These sessions

---

[11] *Grave Talk* (2015). London: Church House Publishing.

can be a good way of enabling people to begin to talk about difficult topics. Consider this situation:

The Mothers' Union attached to the church in a market town meets once a month in the church hall. There are a number of people who attend regularly. There are also a significant number of unchurched or de-churched men and women who attend special and social events. The Mothers' Union have decided to run a Grave Talk event which is to be open to everyone interested. The topic has been chosen in the hope that the material will help and be a blessing to those who attend. There is an awareness that those who come will know that the session is being run by Christians who believe in a God who holds the bigger and longer story, but the focus is on responding to need, using a learning tool that has been tried and tested and found to be useful. The Mother's Union have also decided to advertise the event through the local older people's befriending scheme.

You have agreed to help at this event alongside another more experienced facilitator.

- How do you react to the example?
- What draws you in and what are you resistant to, and why do you think this might be?
- Where have you seen or been involved in similar missional learning in the past?
- What possibilities do you see in your context?
- What skills do you and those you minister with already have or could develop?
- Is there anyone else you could invite to be involved?

Many churches have regular groups that meet together, for example ladies' or men's breakfasts; theological societies; sports and creative groups. These often have special events aimed to attract members of the wider community to serve and bless the community by seeking to help address physical, social, psychological or spiritual needs.

Transforming unjust structures

While, as this book demonstrates, lectures and talks are sometimes a less effective way of enabling learning, they still are popular and many people attend. Consider this situation:

Your local secondary school regularly invites guest speakers to come and talk to those who have just completed their GCSE exams about charities that they are involved in either as volunteers or employees. The speakers are also asked to share what motivates them to be involved in the work. The aim for the school is that the students become more aware of charitable work locally, nationally and globally. You are involved with a local charity and have offered to do a talk for the school about its work. You will need to prepare some slides about the work of the charity and your role. You might also need to decide what you want to share about your faith and how it has led you into this work.

Speaking opportunities often come up for people who have an area of expertise that people want to hear about. In the church context this is often about theology; sometimes practical theology as in the case above, or a more academic theology, for example a series of talks on the Old Testament prophets.

- How do you react to the example?
- What draws you in and what are you resistant to, and why do you think this might be?
- Where have you seen or been involved in similar missional learning in the past?
- What possibilities do you see in your context?
- What skills do you and those you minister with already have or could develop?
- Is there anyone else you could invite to be involved?

Where might opportunities to give a talk, like the one above, be available to you?

Renewing the life of the earth

Small groups can be a helpful way of providing an environment for people to learn. These can be one-off groups, longer term groups or groups that meet for a period of time for a particular purpose. Usually, a facilitator is required to prepare for and lead the group. Consider this situation:

The church-run nursery has asked a number of you who are passionate about environmental issues whether you would be willing to run a weekly small group session over the summer term for an hour for the carers who drop off their children for afternoon care. This is to coincide with some work the nursery is planning to do with the children over the summer on Caring for God's Planet. They have given you the programme of what the children will cover and have asked if you can produce some material for the planned small group. They have about twelve carers who are interested and able to attend, and they are aware that the sessions will be run by the Church.

Small group learning can take many forms, for example, cell groups; home groups; missional communities and reading groups. Small groups learning can take place face-to-face or online.

- How do you react to the example?
- What draws you in and what are you resistant to, and why do you think this might be?
- Where have you seen or been involved in similar missional learning in the past?
- What possibilities do you see in your context?
- What skills do you and those you minister with already have or could develop?
- Is there anyone else you could invite to be involved?

Small groups do require the person leading the group to have some understanding and skills in running small groups. This is the subject of the next chapter.

Takeaways

- Missional learning can take many forms
- Missional learning is context dependent
- Missional learning requires us to listen to God, to our communities and to ourselves
- Missional learning requires us to be flexible and to be willing to be interrupted
- Missional learning is mutual

8. Working with Groups

In this chapter we will explore some of the key elements of working with groups including starting a group, stages of group development, facilitation skills and the roles people play in groups.

What is a group?

At its simplest, a group has three characteristics:
- members
- relationship between the members
- an organising principle

A church congregation could be called a group, but so could three of you meeting together to pray once a week. People join groups because of a common interest or to address a particular need. Groups then generate a network of relationships where roles get established, and values and norms (ways of doing things) emerge.

Groups are an integral part of our lives, from being born into a family to school, church, leisure, interest, work and more. We are all part of groups. They are a building block of society and the way in which tasks are often accomplished. Groups are places where we can become known, develop our skills and abilities and find support. Groups can be both formal or informal and may change constantly as different members come and go.

Starting a group

If you are starting a new group, these are some of the things you may want to consider:
- aims and how it fits with any wider strategy

- practical arrangements: budget, venue, day, time, frequency, duration of sessions and if it is a time-limited group
- recruitment to the group
- leader / facilitator(s) and any training needs
- accountability, record keeping and reviewing

It is vital to put time and energy into the first session of the group. You might want to think about it as birthing a group and all the planning that goes into that. You may also want to think about how you want to establish ground rules. Those leading or facilitating the group might want to think about three messages to communicate in the first session:

- competency – you know what you are doing
- compassion – you demonstrate caring and acceptance to help people feel safe
- commitment – you believe in the group and what it is there for

We may experience group members joining at different times and so want to think about how that can impact the existing group and the importance of trying to reassert these three elements. It is worth noting that to work out the number of different relationships there are in the group you take the number of members, subtract 1 and then multiply the two numbers, and finally divide by 2. For example, in a group of 8 there are 28 one-to-one relationships (8*7 = 56; 56/2 = 28). No wonder groups are complicated!

Stages of group development

One of the most commonly used theories of group development is that of Tuckman.[12] He suggested that there are four key stages of group development: forming, storming, norming, performing. Others

---

[12] Tuckman, B. W. (1965). Developmental sequence in small groups. *Psychological Bulletin, 63*(6), 384-399.

have added a fifth for when groups end called mourning or adjourning.

Forming

The forming stage is when the group comes together and begins to become cohesive. It is a complicated stage and some members of the group may feel tentative about being part of the group and many will have questions. For example, Do I fit? or Is this group for me? Groups can become dependent on a leader (official or unofficial) in the early stages because there are so many uncertainties. Establishing ground rules or boundaries, sometimes known as contracting, very early on can be helpful and put people at ease. Finding ways to get to know each other can also be useful in the early stages, but ensuring that they are context appropriate, comfortable and safe is vital.

As a group facilitator or leader, remember that everyone comes to a new group with experiences of other groups, good and bad, which can influence their engagement in this new one. Each time a new person joins there will be an element of revisiting this forming stage.

Storming

It is really important to remember that this is a normal part of group process and not to get too anxious if it happens to a group we are leading or facilitating. At this stage people are getting to know each other and beginning to let their guard down and possibly testing the boundaries. We might see people acting in different ways, which are not fully conducive to good group functioning, and which might even cause friction or tension. This might be particularly true of Christian groups where any conflict can sometimes feel negative. Trying to create safe spaces and times where people can listen to each other properly is very useful at this stage. Sometimes we may need to facilitate the storming so group members feel safe to disagree and put their perspective forward without feeling they are wrong.

Norming

At this stage the group are moving away from their individual concerns towards a sense of interrelating and focus shifts to the mutual concerns of the group. Group norms, which are the accepted ways of behaving and relating, begin to emerge at this stage. It might be that some of the norms are less than helpful and this needs to be addressed (e.g. if most people arrive late). Negotiation and co-operation continue to be part of what the group does at this stage. There should be a clear sense of working on the task the group was formed for. The more a group gets established, the less a facilitator or leader may need to intervene.

Performing

Performing might begin during the norming stage, but groups should get to a place where there is a clear way that the group works and where tasks are accomplished. At this stage, people feel that they know they fit and may even have established roles. Performing groups require more facilitation than leadership as members of the group take responsibility for the operation of the group. It can be difficult for new people to join at this stage.

Mourning or Adjourning

Groups may have a fixed time limit or be open-ended. However, most groups end at some point. It can be really unhelpful to end a group without providing an opportunity for members to explore some of the emotions they feel, acknowledge achievements and perhaps disappointments. Identifying learning for both individuals and the organization can also be a significant element of this stage. Mallison suggests a five-element process:

- recalling – high points, helpful things, encouragements
- confession – any areas where hurt may have been caused
- thanksgiving – for what has occurred

- hopes for the future – individual or corporate
- farewell[13]

Facilitating a group

We are purposefully using the term facilitating a group rather than leading a group as that is a more helpful term in many contexts. A facilitator is a guide, someone who supports the group as they work together to achieve their purpose. They help the group move forward and develop rather than rigidly dictate. A good facilitator will work towards:

- relationships which help people feel part of a group and that are respectful and trusting
- group members being accountable to one another and individuals taking responsibility
- clear and agreed aims with decisions emerging from a collaborative process
- clear communication and attentive listening
- equal participation among group members

Listening

As a facilitator, there are five types of listening we need to consider:

- what is being said verbally
- what is being communicated through body language
- what is not being said
- the mood of the group
- what we are feeling inside and how that informs what we are doing

---

[13] Mallison, J. (1997). *The Small Group Leader*. London: Scripture Union.

Questions

We will want to be careful about how we phrase questions. We might want to be conscious of the following:

- Using clear language without leading or suggesting the answer

  e.g. What is Matthew writing about in this passage?

- Clarifying contributions when they are not clear

  e.g. Could you put that another way please?

- Redirecting questions to the whole group rather than answering everything yourself?

  e.g. Does anyone else want to say how they respond to this?

Moving on

Knowing how to move the group forward is also a skill to be learned. It is important to make sure that you don't spend too much time on one topic, but also to check the group are ready to move on. To prepare the group to move on you might like to draw in anyone who has not contributed yet. You might ask if there is anything anyone wants to add, or if anyone has a different idea or perspective. Once we have done this, summarising can help the group see where they have got to and can also be the point where we ask for agreement to move to the next task.

Things that can go wrong in facilitation

Everyone will get some things right and some things wrong. We are all learning after all! However, there are some common mistakes that we can try to avoid:

- being over-controlling – a danger if you are inexperienced or nervous
- being over-flexible – groups need boundaries and some direction to maintain momentum
- being too rigid – try to see a plan for a session as a map rather than a definitive route and be prepared to respond to what is happening in the group
- having favourites – while we may naturally find some people easier to get along with than others we need to be fair and inclusive when facilitating groups
- being manipulative – where we can let it look like the group took the decision but we got the outcome we wanted
- pretending to know more than we do – we don't have all the answers and should be happy to admit this, it is role-modelling a mutual learning process
- being over-responsible – the group needs to take responsibility, individually and overall, we also need to remember not to take things personally if things happen that are outside of our control
- wanting to be liked – we all want this, but sometimes, respect is more important

Co-facilitation

Where it is possible, leading a group with someone else works really well. It means that group members see different styles, they see teamwork modelled and if necessary, one of you can deal with issues or emergencies while the other one continues the group facilitation. If you are able to do this, good planning is vital so you both know what each is responsible for and have agreed ground rules as to how you relate in this role. If we are facilitating large groups then we will usually want to find some way of breaking them down into smaller groups, at least for part of the time. We may identify facilitators for these small groups or allow the group to sort it out themselves. Clear instructions are vital, ideally in writing and repeated, as many of us don't pick up what we are being asked to do the first time. It is helpful to have visual ways of recording discussion, decisions, etc. and to ensure that feedback is collated and acted on.

Group behaviour and roles

There are both positive and negative behaviours that we might see in a group; one person might manifest many of them in one session! Negative behaviour is sometimes the consequence of unmet need or arriving at the group with issues or concerns that they are not coping with.

Positive group behaviours	Negative group behaviours
Involving other members	Not listening
Encouraging and praising people	Playing with a phone
Relieving tension	Cutting people off when speaking
Co-operating	Discouraging or deflating comments
Active listening	Picking on people
Sharing information and resources	Inappropriate joking, sarcasm
Elaborating and explaining	Refusal to comply with reasonable requests
Summarizing	Self-pity
Reconciling disagreements	Inappropriate anger or aggression
Giving opinions	Dominating discussions
Starting things	Purposefully difficult body language

Good ground rules and skilled facilitation can minimize some of the negative behaviours and roles in a group although it is usually impossible to eliminate them completely. What is important is to continue to treat people with dignity and respect and not to shame them. Sometimes a private one-to-one might be helpful and at other times the group begins to regulate itself, which can be helpful in establishing that group norms apply to everyone.

Common group roles

Sometimes people can seem to play a role rather than bring their 'real' selves to the discussions. This can be amusing to observe, but can sometimes develop into irritating behaviour and unhealthy scripts. It is good to be aware of this and to encourage people to have the confidence to drop their character and contribute from the heart. These are some of the common characters played:

- **Joker** – may mess around and tell jokes, etc. which can sometimes relieve tension, but may also be disruptive and prevent the group from exploring deeper issues

- **Peacemaker** – tries to bring people together and promote unity, but may be conflict-avoidant and prevent disagreements being explored

- **Encourager** – tries to draw in others and helps with the processes of the group, but there is a danger they may undermine what the facilitator is trying to do

- **Professor** – can contribute useful knowledge-based insights, but may be a little too intellectual and alienate some people

- **Fighter** – can sometimes stand up for those who are feeling marginalized, but may be hostile and defensive and alienate other group members

- **Passive** – sometimes this is how people in groups appear until they are comfortable, but if it continues they may appear withdrawn, disinterested or passively aggressive

- **Dominator** – can be helpful in breaking the ice but needs checking if they don't stop talking, interrupt others or speak without listening

- **Storyteller** – listening to stories is often encouraging and helps us learn, but if someone frequently launches into a 'something similar happened to me' type story it can be distracting and boring

- **Light bulb** – coming up with new ideas can be creative, but doing so endlessly can be distracting and may mean some of the earlier ideas are lost

Takeaways

- Don't automatically blame yourself if a group is not working well; identify the roles people are taking and tweak your approach
- Regularly review the group and your role as a facilitator so you can adjust it in the light of the stage the group is at
- Watch more experienced facilitators and learn from them
- Ensure groups are well planned and that both facilitators and group members know what is happening
- Notice group dynamics (including your own part) and help people move beyond difficult behaviour

9. Working with Individuals

This chapter offers an overview of things to consider in the context of one-to-one (1:1) teaching and learning relationships in the church.

Before you begin reading it you might want to reflect on your own experience of 1:1 relationships within and without the church context. Where have you been the 'teacher' in these relationships? Where have you been the learner? What do you notice?

1:1 teaching and learning relationships take many shapes and forms in the church. Some are informal, for example when friends meet for a drink and, as they talk, there can be learning about God, the world, and themselves. Other teaching and learning relationships are more formal, for example, mentoring, spiritual accompaniment, coaching and tutoring. Some formal 1:1 relationships, like bereavement visiting, are more pastoral than educational in focus and motivation, and yet growth and development is often the result of the work done.

In deciding whether to take on the role of the person *holding the space* for another in a 1:1 relationship, we usually consider a number of questions including:

- Are we called?
- Are we trained?
- Are we prepared?
- Are we supported?
- Are we aware of boundaries and power dynamics?

The titles and descriptions given to 1:1 teaching and learning relationships are important, but can vary significantly in different church contexts. In a similar way, the nature and content of what happens in those relationships can vary depending on the people involved. In this chapter we will consider five kinds of formal 1:1 teaching and learning relationships within the church. The roles fulfilled by Marcella, James, Martha, Ferdia and Mark below serve to give examples of these different relationships. We will then suggest eight areas to consider before embarking on formal 1:1 relationships. These areas can also be used to review the relationship at regular intervals over time.

Marcella and Sandrine:

Sandrine is a new Christian. She attended an Alpha course and is now a regular attender at Bread of Life, a fresh expression of church that takes place in a local cafe. Marcella, an older lady who has been an active Christian for many years, has been asked to mentor Sandrine and meet with her each week to study the book of Mark together. Marcella already mentors another relatively new Christian, and is encouraged to see those she meets with grow in faith through the ups and downs of life. Marcella is supported and supervised in this task by the person heading up the mentoring team. She attended six evening sessions to prepare her for this role.

James and Joshua:

Joshua is a relatively newly ordained church leader. He has moved house to lead a diocesan church plant in a nearby market town. He has a good and supportive team, both where he now lives and with his sending church. He has been meeting with James, a trained coach, every 12 weeks to consider how to move forward in this new environment. Joshua values the structured approach James takes. Rather than telling him what to do, James helps Joshua consider how he and the team he works with can discern God's will, what they want to do and how to do it. James has regular supervision for his work as a coach, and attends ongoing Continuing Professional Development training.

Martha and Lou:

Martha is a spiritual accompanier. She trained for two years for this role. She does this independently, has her own personal insurance and advertises through a national organization of which she is a member. She attends the local Methodist Church. She meets with a supervisor every two months to discuss her role and attends study days in the local area and nationally. She is also part of a peer supervision group. She sees this ministry as a way of enabling people to discern God in their lives and to grow in their relationship with him individually and in community. While she is not teaching, she is providing a space for the person she is accompanying to learn about God, themselves and the world. Martha has been meeting with Lou for over a year. At their next meeting they plan to review the last year and consider whether they both think it is right to continue to meet together for spiritual accompaniment for a further year.

Ferdia and Jon:

Ferdia is a member of her church's Christian Listener team. She trained for this role with Acorn a number of years ago. She meets with people who want the space just to talk and be listened to. She is aware that this is a listening role and not counselling. It isn't teaching either, but it is a deep place of learning. She appreciates seeing the way that God works and how healing and growth take place as she listens. Ferdia has met with Jon three times following his redundancy at work which hit him quite badly. He has found that space to be listened to has helped him begin to cope with what has happened, to reconnect with God and to start to consider how to face the future. He has now linked in with the local Job Centre, which he couldn't face when they first met. Every six months the listening team participate in a group supervision session.

Mark:

Mark is a parish minister in the Church of England. He is a Training Incumbent (TI) which means he sometimes has a curate with him for a period of up to three years. The curate has completed some training before being ordained and is now learning to put this into practice. This was traditionally very much an apprenticeship model where the TI was seen as the master craftsman and the curate the apprentice – but things are changing. In fact, sometimes a curate can know more about some areas of ministry than their TI does. Mark's last curate had been a reader for 25 years and had taught Mark a lot about liturgy. Mark met with his curate once a week as a supervisor. This was to help ensure that his curate learned what was required before taking on their own post. Sometimes he had to give the curate a short tutorial on a subject, like taking funerals or doing the paperwork (or online forms) for a wedding. Mark also meets on a one-to-one basis with other curates from different parishes as a theological reflector to give them space to reflect on what they have been experiencing and learning. Sadly, he has not been trained for any of these roles properly and he does not receive supervision for them.

Areas to consider

In the next section we look at eight areas to consider in the context of 1:1 teaching and learning relationships in the church and pose some questions.

1. Role

   What is the role? This gives clarity to both of the participants in the 1:1 relationship and sets clear boundaries for what is expected of it. It is often worth trying to sum this up in one sentence.

2. Calling

   Do I feel called to this role? A need doesn't necessarily constitute a call. It is important to take time to consider whether this is God's calling for you at this time. Are you feeling pressured into it by others, or by yourself, for other reasons? It is also important to be aware that sometimes life happens and we need, for our own self-care, to step out of teaching and learning relationships for a period of time. One way of discerning this is asking whether you feel called to faithful prayer for the person that you are meeting with.

3. Training

Have I been trained for this role? Most formal roles need some form of training. The nature of training, assessment and ongoing development required will depend on the role. Mark has been very unhappy with the lack of training for his role as a supervisor and as a theological reflector. He has raised this a number of times, but nothing so far has been done. He has therefore decided to complete a year-long course on pastoral supervision. He is not sure how he will keep this training up-to-date yet, but expects that the organisation which is doing the training will be able to signpost him to this after he completes the course.

4. Accountability

To whom am I accountable? In formal 1:1 roles in the church, where there is a power differential, consistent, open and transparent accountability is important as we seek to ensure good pastoral practice. There should be a named person for this and clear and explicit processes for raising of concerns.

5. Supervision

Do I need supervision for this role? When we are involved in formal 1:1 teaching and learning relationships, supervision, a protected time to confidentially reflect with a trained supervisor on issues relating to the role, is essential. Sometimes this is provided within the local church. Sometimes, as with Martha's peer supervision, this is provided on a diocesan or regional basis. Sometimes, as in the case of James, who is a business coach, this has to be found outside the local and regional church structures.

6. Safeguarding

Do I need safeguarding training and a DBS check? Power dynamics come into play in all 1:1 relationships whether we perceive it or not. We may also be working with vulnerable adults or adults who become vulnerable for a period of time. Your safeguarding team can assess what level of training you need and tell you how to access it. They will also be able to offer advice about whether a DBS check is necessary.

7. What are the boundary issues?

There are many boundary issues to consider in 1:1 relationships. Boundaries are there to keep everyone safe and when they are infringed or crossed it is important to consider why and what needs to be done about it. This is where supervision can help. Some boundary issues to consider are:

a. Where will you meet and is this a safe space for you both? A room which has a glass door in the church centre is a confidential but open space. A wooden door would make this a closed space and might potentially disguise inappropriate behaviours or allow false accusations.

b. When will you meet, how often and for how long? Time is a significant boundary and clarity protects both parties. When meetings planned for an hour regularly last longer, or when one party keeps cancelling or arriving late, or when meetings become more frequent, there are boundary problems.

c. Dual roles. As well as being her mentor, Marcella will meet Sandrine in other church contexts. How is this going to be negotiated? Is the mentoring relationship something that everyone knows about?

d. This also leads on to the issue of confidentiality and its limits. Safeguarding training will make the rare reasons for breaking confidentiality very explicit and will guide how this needs to be done. However, the expectation in most 1:1 teaching and learning relationships is that confidentiality is retained. Jon does not expect Ferdia to share what he says to her with anyone else.

e. Other boundary issues to consider are the place of touch; the importance of mutuality; the dangers of over-involvement and how our emotions can impact on each other in different ways. What we wear and what we share of ourselves are also boundary issues, as is the issue of giving and receiving of gifts and money, which can include who pays for the coffee if we meet in a private part of a local cafe. Underpinning all this is the boundary issue of self-care. This is about self-care of ourselves in and for the teaching and learning role. We do need a balanced and healthy pattern of life that roots us securely in God.

8. Power

What do I need to know about power dynamics? The first thing is to realise that there are power dynamics in all relationships. There are also power dynamics in the context in which those relationships take place. For example, an able-bodied organization that fails to recognize the needs of those with specific learning needs creates an uneven playing field. A predominantly white patriarchal organization can, even unconsciously, disadvantage those who do not fit the organizational norms. The more a learner does not 'fit in', the more disadvantaged and disempowered they are likely to be. For example, someone with less income may be unable to easily get to the rural retreat house to meet as they do not have a car and cannot afford the taxi fare.

If prayer is part of the 1:1 teaching and learning relationship, even that can become a demonstration of power when what is prayed for becomes a form of manipulation or control.

Reflecting on power in 1:1 teaching and learning relationships is therefore essential. There are many different ways of understanding power in relationships. The questions below encourage us to consider, as teachers and learners, what power we have and inhabit. It will vary in each 1:1 teaching and learning context.

a. What is your position in the church? Even the title of 'Christian Listener' conveys a role, a title and maybe a badge. This is position power. Uniforms are another way of displaying positional power, for example by Mark wearing his dog collar.

b. How does your character and the way you interact with people influence them? Power is about influence, and we need to be aware how the person we are impacts on others. Sandrine may begin to put Marcella on a pedestal, and be influenced by Marcella in other areas of her life, for example in her approach to child care. This is a manifestation of charismatic and relational power.

c. How are your skills and abilities valued by the organisation? Expertise and experience results in power. For example, Mark has his experience as an ordained minister and Martha as a spiritual accompanier.

d. Sometimes in 1:1 relationships, people have the power to reward people. This can be quite subtle or more obvious. For example, James may be in a position, due to another role in the wider organisation, to recommend or prevent Joshua from being offered other more prominent roles. This is reward power.

e. Power can arise from knowing about processes and how things work. Martha knows and understands the normal processes for spiritual accompaniment; for example the idea that after an initial three meetings the relationship would normally be reviewed by the person being accompanied and accompanier together to see if it is right to continue meeting. She knows it would be good practice to review this on an annual basis. She has information power, which she can share or withhold.

The biggest problem with power is pretending that it doesn't exist. We need to be aware of power dynamics, and cultivate the desire and ability to avoid having inappropriate power over others. Making issues of power and vulnerability in the relationship and context explicit can help. Regular review of the relationship and seeking feedback from the learner which results in change, can empower and give the learner voice.

You might find it helpful to consider or even complete the table below for the different 1:1 relationships you are involved in.

Role	What is the role and what are its limits?
Calling	Why do I feel called to this role?
Training	What training have I had for this and how will I keep my skills and knowledge up to date?
Accountability	To whom am I accountable? How can the person I am in the teaching and learning relationship with raise concern? Do they know this?
Supervision	What supervision do I have in place for this role?
Safeguarding	Is my safeguarding training up to date and at the right level? Do I know the local safeguarding contact details and processes?
Boundaries	What are the obvious boundary issues? What are the less obvious boundary issues? What has been agreed about the 1:1 teaching and learning relationship with the person concerned and with the organisation / church?

Power	What are the issues of power and vulnerability? How is the learner being empowered? What power do I have as the person 'holding the space'? What contextual issues disempower the learner?

Takeaways

- Be sure that the nature and boundaries of the 1:1 relationship are clear and understood
- Be aware of and consider the specific issues relating to power and vulnerability in each relationship
- Ensure clear and transparent accountability structures and processes
- Ensure supervision and appropriate insurance is in place
- Ensure that you are and remain trained for the role

10. Barriers to Learning

There are all sorts of barriers to learning, some of which we have touched on in earlier chapters.

Physical exclusion

The most obvious barrier is physical accessibility. If a person cannot be there to participate because of timing, location or problems of accessibility with either building or technology, then they are effectively barred from the learning activity. Then there is the suitability of the place when they get there. Are the internal facilities accessible to people with different physical needs? Is it equipped with sound loop, etc.? Also, more mundanely, but still important, is the environment comfortable? Does it have toilet facilities? Is there fresh air? Is it well lit? Are people seated on stable chairs with sufficient personal space?

This needs both sensitivity to potential barriers and practical removal of them.

Lack of confidence

Some adult learners have had bad experiences as children; perhaps they were frightened by the teachers, or humiliated when they made a mistake. Others may have been told that they were not very good at things, or not very clever, or did not feel able to engage in a competitive environment. Some may have tried learning as an adult and felt that their efforts were a waste of time or money. They need encouragement to engage with confidence and lots of help and reassurance that they belong and are doing well.

Social barriers

People may shy away from learning because of internalised stereotypes of what learners should look like, i.e. not like me! They may feel that they are too old, too young, too working class, too practical, etc. Again, this may come from difficult childhood experiences and enculturation. For example, being told that 'people like us don't stay on at school', 'you are not as clever as your sister', 'earning is better than learning', etc.

Genuine valuing of different gifts, insights, experiences and background in the learning process, alongside careful attention to different learning styles, will be both healing and liberating.

Fear of looking silly

All learning requires some recognition and readjustment of what we already know. Whilst some people will boldly ask questions, others may be nervous of admitting they do not know something that seems obvious. This can be especially true of people who have been attending church for a long time, but who have never really examined their faith in any great detail. 'After twenty years I should know this … admitting I don't will make me look silly!'

When facilitating learning, it is important to demonstrate that we don't know everything ourselves, to ask questions and learn from the participants, and to repeat often, 'There is no such thing as a silly question!'.

Material and methods

However hard we try, sometimes when we get there, the material and methods just don't somehow seem to work. It may be that we have pitched things too basic or too advanced or too narrowly. It may be that a new group is not yet confident enough to join in with some of the more creative activities. It may be that we have misunderstood what they were really hoping for from the sessions. Although this can be hard, it may also be that they do not have confidence in you as a learning facilitator (yet!).

All these things can feel really awkward, but are actually quite easily addressed. Just ask the group what is wrong. This is a very powerful way of demonstrating how adult education is mutual. If necessary, explain you are facilitating their learning and not trying to prove yourself to be an expert. Make any necessary adjustments to materials and methods needed going forward. A less direct way of doing this is to use an exercise like the one below.

Mindy was wondering how to talk about the dynamics in her group. Things didn't seem quite right and when she tried to chat to a couple of the members they insisted everything was fine. She then remembered an exercise she had done at college where all the class had to draw and colour themselves as a fish, place the fish in the ocean picture the teacher had created and then explain to the class why they had drawn the fish as they had and then why they had placed it in the picture as they did. This had led to a much greater understanding about how the group saw themselves and each other and enabled some more open conversation about how the class related.

Cost

Cost need not necessarily be monetary, although that is often the case. Even if there is no charge for the learning itself, if a person has to take time off work, or pay to get there or for childcare, then finances can be a barrier. There may be conscious or unconscious encouragement or expectation that learners should buy books or equipment to assist them and further their learning, which leads some people to drop out. Even going out for a coffee together afterwards may be a financial strain for some.

Again, sensitivity to possible problems and discrete help is needed. This need not be monetary. Asking people to share lifts, providing a creche and checking out most convenient times to meet will help. If extra resources are recommended then try to find ones that are freely available and if possible, provide refreshments.

Difficult group dynamics

As we saw in Chapter 8, there are many different dynamics at play in a group. If these get out of hand then they can become a barrier to others. For example, if an individual continually brings attention back to themselves, or jumps in with a closed answer before others have chance to contribute, or changes the conversation back to their pet subject. Also, small cliques within the larger group can cause problems if they chat inappropriately whilst learning is happening or make unkind comments about other people in the group. This is tough to deal with, but again being gently direct is the best course of action. Usually, peer pressure will deal with the problem before too long and in the meantime, you can mitigate by mixing up the group to do work in alternating pairs.

The examples above are of barriers that might be present in any kind of adult learning. When it comes to faith, however, there are particular problems and potential pitfalls that it is good to be aware of.

Faith matters

Facilitating learning about faith brings with it some issues that are really quite different to dealing with other subjects. To begin with, faith is not just something we make logical deductions about. It affects our self-understanding and the way we see others, our behaviour, the way we seek to shape our lives and what decisions we make about our futures. Since any sort of learning involves some unlearning and resetting of our worldview there are some big stakes at play. What if we learn that something we have been sure about and lived by in the past is wrong, or more complicated than we thought?

Furthermore, different people see learning about faith in different ways. Take for example learning about scripture. Some people read scripture and take proof texts from it and will be keen that others learn these texts and their implications. Others will be interested in the historical and socio-economic background of scripture and want to explore how the truths contained in scripture might be applied to contemporary contexts. Others will want to engage spiritually with scripture and approach it through meditation and contemplation. Others will take a more detached view of scripture and want to critique it.

Then there is the question of different faith traditions, and whether scripture, experience, tradition or reason is prioritised as a start and end point for learning. In addition to intellectual resistance when exploring different perspectives to our own there may also be emotional resistance. For example, there may be a tendency towards deference to faith leaders, which can lead to passivity and resistance to learning an alternative perspective. Often, usually unconsciously, people learn theology from Bible stories they encounter as a child and the hymns they know and sing. This is a particular sort of learning that is emotionally very deep rooted in a person. The literalistic childhood memory may feel stronger and more 'real' and the hymns may become associated with social belonging. It can be extremely difficult to deal with the consequences of bringing this type of faith into question as it may engender fear or guilt or both.

All of this may well be connected with personality and preferences as explored above, but it certainly complicates matters!

Again, the best way to address the issues is to talk about them. Allow space for people to think and talk through any learning about their faith that disrupts their worldview and self-understanding. Explain the different ways of approaching scripture and be mindful of how you and the group see things, especially when they are different. If it is the right thing to do, introduce different approaches and perspectives gently and prayerfully. Remind people that although exploring faith might lead to them to change some of their views about God, God won't break and desires a relationship with us based on real trust and deepening understanding.

It may be helpful to share stories of how peoples' faith has changed, within the group, or to look at the faith journeys of various saints, pioneers of social justice and religious leaders. There are also a number of metaphors that it might be helpful to discuss when it comes to accepting that faith changes. For example, inner journey, outward growth, death and resurrection, mountain top and valleys, creative unfolding, sanctification, grace, yearning for God, authenticity and religious maturity, etc.

Specific theories of how faith changes over time

It can also be helpful to remember that faith changes over time in response to learning. Below are some theories of how that happens.

Name	Theory	Summary	Reference
James Fowler	Faith Development Theory	Faith passes through seven distinct phases over a lifespan due to natural maturation: 0. Undifferentiated 1. Intuitive-Projective 2. Mythic-Literal 3. Synthetic-Conventional 4. Individuative-Reflective 5. Conjunctive 6. Universalising.	Fowler, J. W. (1981). *Stages of Faith: the psychology of human development.* San Francisco, CA: Harper & Row.

Name	Theory	Summary	Reference
		The stages are presented as hierarchical and it is claimed very few adults move beyond stage 3.	
Carol Gilligan	In a Different Voice	A critique of Fowler exploring how young women's moral development is influenced by relationships, feelings of care and responsibility and how their actions will affect others.	Gilligan, C. (1993). *In a Different Voice: psychological theory and women's development.* Harvard University Press.
Nicola Slee	Women's Faith Development Theory	Women's faith development is connected with their whole lives and has six processes: 1. Conversational 2. Metaphoric 3. Narrative 4. Personalised 5. Conceptual 6. Apophatic. There are also three patterns: 1. Alienation 2. Awakening 3. Relationality.	Slee, N. (2004). *Women's Faith Development: patterns and processes.* Aldershot: Ashgate.

Name	Theory	Summary	Reference
Heinz Streib	Religious Styles	Change in representation of faith is prompted by social interaction and moves through five stages: 1. Subjective 2. Instrumental-reciprocal 3. Mutual 4. Individuative-systemic 5. Dialogical.	Streib, H. (2001). 'Faith development theory revisited: The religious styles perspective.' *The International Journal for the Psychology of Religion*, 11(3), 143-58.
John Westerhoff	Theory of Faith Enculturation	Change in faith via social and environmental interactions moving through four stages: 1. Experienced 2. Affiliative 3. Searching 4. Owned.	Westerhoff III, J. H. (1976). *Will Our Children Have Faith?* New York, NY: Seabury.

Takeaways

- Think carefully about what barriers potential learners might experience
- Try to create a relaxed atmosphere
- Actively encourage and value different views
- Remember that everyone begins from a different understanding and experience of faith
- Remember that faith changes over time in response to learning, life and encounter of difference

11. What Could Go Wrong?

The answer to this question is as broad as it is long. Some hiccups are more usual than others, but there is always space for surprise...

- You turn up to the venue for the teaching session which is usually open and it is locked and no-one can be contacted to get the keys

- You discover at the last minute that there is a double booking and half the people who were going to be at the session you were leading need to be somewhere else

- You arrive at the venue and the person who was bringing refreshments has had to go the hospital

- You are having a mentoring session in a local cafe when another friend approaches and draws up a chair to join you

- You get your dates in the diary muddled up and miss a session with your trainee

Many of us are used to risk assessments, both formal and informal. They are basically a way of actively thinking about what could go wrong so that we can minimise the risk of it actually happening. For example, we might identify potential hazards, ask who could be hurt, and decide what action should be taken to minimise the risk. The venues in which we have teaching and learning events usually need to have a completed risk assessment, which will include consideration of what could go wrong with the space, the equipment, the activity and the people.

When we are leading a teaching and learning event, we need to make sure a venue risk assessment has been completed, but we also need to consider more widely what could go wrong. For example, what could go wrong at an evening Lent Course?

St George's church is doing a Lent course on Global Poverty. Fifteen people have signed up to meet in the church hall from 7.30pm - 9.00pm every Wednesday evening in Lent. Each session will start with coffee and biscuits. There is an up-to-date risk assessment for the venue in the church office. The facilitator wants to consider what else could go wrong beyond what is covered in the venue risk assessment.

One way of addressing this is to do a mind map using paper or a mind map app on the computer. In the centre of it write the question: what could go wrong? Then mind map it, giving it five initial branches, for example, prayer, the planned learning, the environment, the people and other issues. Then add further branches. Identify how each risk might be minimized, and/or addressed if it happens.

Another way of producing a risk assessment is to use a table format. The beauty of this is that it can become a check list that can be added to as time goes on. An example is offered below.

Issue	What could happen	Examples	How to address
Prayer	Lack of prayer support	People are not aware of event or of the value of prayer support	
Environ-ment	Access issues	No keys or wheelchair access	
	Furniture issues	Not appropriate to needs	
	Temperature	Too hot or cold	

Issue	What could happen	Examples	How to address
	Hidden conflicting messages	Does the environment reinforce or undermine the teaching?	
	Lack of / wrong refreshments	Allergies; person responsible cannot come	
	Booking issues	Double booking	
	IT hardware / connectors issues	Wrong connectors, plugs in the wrong place	
People	Illness	Facilitator becomes unwell	
	Illness	Group member becomes unwell	
	Lone working issues	In setting up and drawing down	
	Attendance	Only one person comes	
	Attendance	Twice as many as expected come	
	Attendance	People don't come to every session	
Learning	Learning needs	No learning needs identified in the area	
	Learning provision	Already being provided elsewhere locally	

Issue	What could happen	Examples	How to address
	Learning methods	Don't reflect the preferences of those attending	
Other issues	Local events	A local significant event resonates with the area being considered	
	Life happens	A death in the community	
	Life happens	A closed car park	
	Life happens	Road works and diversions impacting on arrival time	
	Life happens	Lack of facilitator preparation time and self-care	

Takeaways

- Consider what could go wrong in relation to the learning, the people and the environment
- Consider what other wider problems could arise
- Do a risk assessment
- Have contingency plans in place
- Review the event formally afterwards and decide what changes are needed for next time

12. How Did It Go?

One of the recurring themes in this book is that of reflecting on and reviewing our experiences. It is important that we reflect on our own learning as teachers and facilitators and consider what could be improved. Sometimes we get formal or informal feedback to help us in this process. In any case we can do an evaluation ourselves.

Whether we are giving a talk, leading a small group or mentoring on a 1:1 basis, it is good to look back and reflect on what happened. In doing this we consider things in the wider context. We ask God to give us insight as we look at it in the light of scripture and our journey of faith. We may, with due regard to confidentiality, talk with a supervisor or colleague about it. We then consider and plan how we might approach a similar situation next time.

In this chapter we are going to consider giving and receiving feedback and evaluation.

The situations

Salome: *Salome is a young adult who is involved in leading a young peoples' group. Last month saw the group lead a service for the whole of the church community and Salome gave the talk in the service. She has asked a number of the church members to fill in a form to give her feedback on this talk, but is not too sure what questions to put on the form. She will also be meeting with Jassica, one of the ministers in the church, for face-to-face feedback.*

New Life Community Church: *New Life Community Church have received local funding to help support a parenting course for those* *living in a new housing estate. They have been asked to complete an evaluation of the course for the funders.*

Feedback

Feedback is essential to learning. Feedback helps identify and clarify what has worked well and in doing so affirms and reinforces good practice. It can also help identify what perhaps has not worked so well, and why. Feedback can help us to evaluate our motivations and methods, promoting self-awareness, and enabling insight. It ideally also offers creative ideas of what to try next time, to assist improvement and growth.

Feedback forms

Feedback can be gathered and received in different ways. Many of us are used to feedback forms. Some of these may ask a question like: how happy were you with the service you received today? We may then face a scale of numbers from 0-10 and have to put a ring round the number that fits with our view of the service received. Sometimes, rather than numbers, smiley faces are used, moving from a very sad face through to a very happy one. These kind of feedback questionnaires are quick and easy, but they are of limited value if they don't tell you why someone has scored a ten or circled a not very happy face. Questionnaires with open questions can be much more helpful.

Rather than a numerical scale or a scale of smiley faces, which will not tell Salome very much about what people thought and felt about her talk, she could instead ask the following:
- What was/were the most important thing/s you gleaned from listening to the talk today?
- Identify two or three things the person giving the talk did well
- What two or three things could have been done differently?
- Are there any other comments you would like to make?

In doing this Salome finds out what people have gained by listening. Some learning points may well be ones she expected and indeed hoped for, but she will also find out the kind of things God has been doing that she was not expecting at all. Salome will get some positive feedback. Positive feedback is important as it will help her know what has particularly helped those who have been listening, especially if they are of different ages and come from many different places, perspectives and backgrounds to herself. Because Salome has made herself vulnerable in asking for feedback, it is good to have at least as many positive points as suggestions for doing things differently. The space for any other comments may bring to light connections with wider life of the listener and the church community and is always helpful in capturing things we have not thought of.

Salome and Jassica would ideally decide together to whom they should give the feedback sheets for completion, as for some it will be a distraction from worship, whereas for others it would be something they would enjoy. It is good to get feedback from a range of different people. Although anonymity can sometimes be helpful, it is more often better to have the name of the person giving the feedback on the form so that clarification or further details can be asked for.

Salome and Jassica can then meet to discuss the feedback forms, reflect on the experience of giving the talk in context, and identify common threads and key learning points. This will help Salome as she prepares to give a talk in the future. Jassica, if she is open and receptive to learning in all situations, is also very likely to learn something worthwhile that will impact on her own practice.

Giving and receiving feedback

Jassica might also give Salome 1:1 feedback. In doing this, it is important to remember some key characteristics of good feedback:

T – it is Timely
E – it is Evidence-based
A – it is Appropriate
M – it is Manageable.[14]

Time should be put aside to give and receive the feedback in a safe environment. The feedback ideally needs to be evidence-based and specific. The acronym PEE can help here: Point, Explanation, Example. A Point is made with an Example to illustrate that point and an Explanation as to why it is seen to be important.

Feedback is about support and challenge. In any given feedback there can be high or low levels of challenge and support. Feedback needs to be adjusted for the person receiving the feedback at that time and the context in which it is happening. The table below gives some examples of different combinations of these.

High challenge **High support**	**High challenge** **Low support**
Thanks so much for that sermon. It really helped me – particularly the challenge to spend time in the Psalms – but you were 10 minutes overtime again.	The sermon was just too long – everyone was getting bored. You are going to have to do something about the timing.
Low challenge **High support**	**Low challenge** **Low support**
I liked the use of illustrations and the way you explored the different peoples' perspectives in the sermon.	Whatever!

---

[14] Rhona Knight, 'Giving and receiving feedback'. In Hastings, A. & Redsell, S. (eds.) (2006). *The Good Consultation Guide for Nurses*. Abingdon: Radcliffe Publishing.

While 'high challenge, low support' feedback may be appropriate in an ongoing, long term, supportive relationship, 'high support, low challenge' is often more appropriate when the learner is in a more vulnerable position.

One approach to feedback that Jassica could use, after ensuring the appropriate environment and time, would be to ask Salome what she thought she did well, and then to tell Salome what she thought had been done well. Then Jassica could ask Salome what she might do differently next time, and then tell Salome her own thoughts on this. This form of feedback is about judgement on behaviours and actions. There is a danger, however, that the affirmation gets lost in the discussions of what might be done differently, resulting in loss of confidence and destabilisation.

Another, less challenging, more time consuming, but often more effective approach is for Jassica to use observational feedback. This is based on feeding back to the learner observed behaviours and words without evaluating them. This is not about 'good' and 'bad'. It simply explores what the person did and why the person thinks they were doing what they were doing. It asks them to consider what they were hoping to achieve and to consider if they achieved this. It then explores other possible ways of approaching what they were aiming for.

> **Jassica:** 'Salome, I noticed that you opened your talk asking people to get into twos and discuss something good that had happened the previous week and then there was a noticeable noise of chattering and laughter in the room.'

> **Salome:** 'I noticed that as well. I had wanted to get people to begin thinking about God's blessing as I was going to be talking about thankfulness. The chattering and laughter seemed to be a sign that asking then to do this had achieved the aim. I also noticed that when people stopped talking and

came back to listen to me there were more smiles on their faces and there was a lighter feel in the room ... it was as if the way had been prepared for me to talk about being thankful.'

Jassica: 'How else might you have achieved this?'

Salome: 'I suppose I could have asked everyone to take a moment and note down some things to be thankful for ... mmmm ... maybe I could have had a time of open thanksgiving prayer?'

Jassica: 'Yes – these two approaches could be useful but I don't think it would have enabled the connection and friendship that seemed to emerge from the approach you used – or the feeling of joy in the room... I did also notice that a couple of people didn't join in.'

Salome: 'Yes, that's right. Maybe nothing good had happened to them the previous week. It might have been an idea for me to have said something like "share something good that has happened in the last week, and if that is not possible something small to be thankful for. And if you would prefer to just be alone or talk alone to God please do that".'

This approach to feedback is not about judging what was good or bad or right or wrong. It is about looking at what happened and assessing its impact; considering what is being aimed for and identifying other possible ways of getting there. In addition, Jassica and Salome will both learn things that they had not planned to, that they can apply in the future.

Kirkpatrick Evaluation Model

In the business and training world, a helpful four-level model is sometimes used to evaluate a learning programme or event. This model comes out of the work of Kirkpatrick.[15] While it is difficult, and indeed often not desirable or practical, to evaluate at all four levels in the local church context, consideration of the different levels can be helpful in designing and delivering teaching and learning programmes. It is also important to remember that evaluating for example a person's relationship with God and growth into the likeness of Christ is of immense kingdom value but not measurable.

Level 1 – Reaction

This is about how much people have liked and engaged with the learning. It is looked at using feedback sheets – also known as happy sheets – remember the smiling faces? In the case of the parenting course at New Life Community Church, a feedback sheet with smiling faces asking questions about how much the course was enjoyed, how much participants felt that they learned and how good the environment and refreshments were would help evaluate at Level 1.

Level 2 – Learning

This is about the learning itself. Earlier in the book we have written about aims and objectives in teaching and learning. These should state what the person engaging with the learning should know or be able to do after completing the learning. Assessments are often used to ascertain if these have been achieved in formal educational and training settings. In the case of the parenting course at New Life Community Church, an open feedback sheet where the participants are asked to identify what they have learned would be a possible way to partially address this. Another possible way would be to devise a creative group or individual activity at the final session that demonstrates what learning has taken place.

---

[15] Kirkpatrick, J. D. & Kirkpatrick, W. K. (2016). *Kirkpatrick's Four Levels of Training Evaluation*. Association for Talent Development.

Level 3 – Behaviour

This is about assessing behaviours. We may have learned how to do something but that does not mean we will do it. Evaluation here involves observing behaviours over a period of time to see if what has been learned is being applied. For example, in the case of the parenting course, one of the aims might have been that those attending would know how to, and be able to, access the local food bank. Knowing how many of the people on the course then accessed the food bank would be a way of evaluating at Level 3. However, this is not always easy to do. In this case it would require consent from the participants to look at and record their personal data. It also turns course participants into research subjects – a significant change – and may compromise the nature of the learning. Careful discernment is needed to assess appropriate assessments!

Level 4 – Results

This is about assessing the result of learning. Has the learning produced the desired results? In the context of a parenting course this is again difficult to assess. Parenting aims and objectives are about long-term, rather than short-term, gains.

Evaluating course material or the impact of its use elsewhere may sometimes be an alternative way of evidencing the benefit of a course to funders.

Takeaways

- Seek feedback on teaching and learning events
- Reflect on the learning experience and feedback and adapt practice in the light it
- Feedback can be observational – noticing what happened and what happened next
- Feedback can be evaluative – what was good and what is in need of development

- Giving feedback needs to be Timely, Evidence-based, Appropriate and Manageable

13. An Introduction to Theological Reflection

We reflect on what happens to us as part of our desire for meaning and understanding. As we reflect we aim to develop and improve and look to do things differently another time. As Christians, we then look to bring our faith into this reflection. The outcome can shape the way we do things in the future, including facilitating groups.

There are a wide range of approaches to theological reflection, but the task can be summarized as having six main elements:

- Identifying experiences to reflect on
- Making connections with our context and culture
- Asking where is God in this situation or experience?
- Making connections with Christian tradition, theology and the Bible
- Drawing these insights together
- Taking action or moving on from where we started and integrating the new knowledge or insight into practice, attitudes, frames of reference, etc.

One of the early pioneers of theological reflection in a UK context was Laurie Green who worked it out in an urban context. The congregation would probably not have thought of themselves as theologians – but they were! Green talks about a pastoral spiral, which suggests a dynamism to the process where you start next time from where you finished last time.[16] The diagram on the next page summarises his approach.

---

[16] Green, L. (1990). *Let's Do Theology: a pastoral cycle resource book*. London: Continuum.

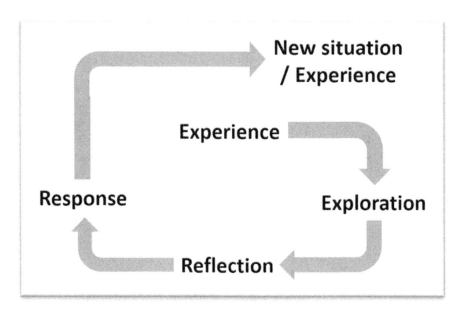

There are many resources that you can use in theological reflection and it may be that in learning contexts you want to use a variety and get participants focusing on one element to reflect on rather than necessarily drawing on all the suggested elements each time. This would usually take too long as part of a group exercise. *Tools for Reflective Ministry* by Sally and Paul Nash has practical suggestions for many different tools you can use for reflection including metaphor, spiritual practices, reframing, culture, not using words, nature and group approaches.[17]

In the appendices are a Learning Checklist, which lists the questions which should be asked in preparation for a learning session and an Example Learning Checklist showing how this may be filled in.

The appendices also contain an Example Teaching Session Outline for a short course entitled 'An Introduction to Mark'. We have imagined how Session 1 may have gone and the Table below shows what issues

---

[17] Nash, S. & Nash, P. (2006). *Tools for Reflective Ministry*. London: SPCK.

Green's theological reflection model could have raised for the facilitator as they reflected upon how the session went.

Experience	9 people came to the first of our three part series introducing Mark's gospel, 12 had expressed interest. One leader pulled out last minute as their child was ill leaving 2 of us to run the programme and pick up their elements. Timing largely worked.
What happened and how do I feel about it?	Arriving 30 mins early wasn't quite enough to set up the room as we wanted to and to get refreshments ready for the break as people arrived early and we wanted to be able to welcome them well. People liked being given their own copy of Mark's gospel for the course. We forgot to buy some non-dairy milk. Singing didn't work brilliantly as Sam who couldn't come is the one of us who can sing! Had to improvise a bit to cover Sam's input as we didn't have their notes. Odd number meant we put people in 3s not pairs for discussion. Choosing the image of Jesus was interesting but not enough time for everyone to feedback. Need more images and to spend more time on it (see * in Response section below). Generally felt fairly happy but a bit frustrated with a couple of things I should have thought about and got right. Felt a bit disappointed that Dan didn't come, he seemed so enthusiastic on Sunday. Didn't really know what to do when Jane told Will they were wrong about the end of the gospel. Need to have a strategy for dealing with unhelpful comments, perhaps we need some ground rules.

Exploration	Big football match tonight on TV may have influenced attendance for one or two.
What in our context may have influenced this? How were people when they came to the session? How was I feeling?	Didn't send reminder on What'sApp group – hadn't agreed who was going to do that so didn't get done. May be needed to do more one to one inviting or reminding on Sunday. Not everyone seems to listen to the notices! Dark and rainy which might impact one or two people. Need system for asking for lifts. Bit of a mix of mood as people arrived, a couple looked really tired, probably three of them were positively anticipating opportunity for study. Not sure about others. Perhaps a theme rather than a whole gospel might have been of more interest to some for a short course. Maybe we could get some feedback on what people would like a short course on for the next one! I think I was a bit nervous which meant I was really focused on what I was saying rather than seeing the responses, etc. and very conscious of wanting to finish on time which perhaps meant I closed down some helpful discussion.
Reflection	Felt a deep sense of peace when I prayed about the meeting and felt that I should be trusting God and not worrying about my skills at group facilitation but to try to do what I had been asked to do as well as I could. Those verses in Matthew 6 about not worrying came to mind. Then the bit in Matthew 10 about all who are weary and heavy laden coming to Jesus as he will give you rest. I think I have been taking too much on myself and expecting everything to be brilliant first off.
Did we sense anything when we prayed about this? What in my faith experience relates to this e.g. Bible, songs,	

theology, books, podcasts, etc.	Occurred to me it may be good to have some quiet music playing as people arrive to give a sense of peace. I also thought about the story of Mary and Martha in Luke 10 where Mary is commended for sitting and listening to Jesus but I know I was much more like Martha, running around trying to make sure everything was right. I know there are things to be done but must remember what is most important. I am thinking about the incarnation and how this course will help me understand more about Jesus and what it meant for God to become a human. The final thing that came to mind as I was reflecting on this was that it's not just down to me – I am part of the body of Christ and I need to do my bit and everyone else their bit!
Response In the light of all the experience, exploration and reflection, what do we need to do? What does God now expect us?	Practically: Send a reminder out via Church WhatsApp for next session on the day, arrive 45 minutes early to give time to set up, buy non-dairy milk, tweak the timings so enough time for the final reflection, agree some ground rules. Ensure we send all the leaders anything for our input 24 hours before session so easier to pick something up if someone drops out. God: pray and trust God that the right people will attend but make sure that we do our part in asking. Pray for the strength of the Holy Spirit as I deliver my parts. Reflect on my growing understanding of who Jesus is and what the incarnation means. Create a welcoming hospitable space where we listen to each other but can have different opinions and perspectives.

	Remember to get the Martha and Mary balance right between being and doing and let everyone do their parts and me do mine. * One option would be to use the Methodist Collection of Modern Art[18] images of Jesus and ask which one they think most closely represents the Jesus of Mark's gospel they have encountered tonight. People may be given the opportunity to share why they chose a particular image. What hopefully might happen another time is that we reflect on our experience, explore the different images there, reflect on what the different images say to each of us, respond by choosing one and everyone has fresh insights into how we might see Jesus in Mark. Furthermore, as several people share we also learn that we all perceive things differently and that there is not one 'right' way to see Jesus.
New situation Where am I starting from next time?	Be more secure that we are well planned and organized for the session and go into session 2 having tweaked what needed improving in session 1. Hopefully now trusting God more, realizing I am part of a team and focusing on my part in what we are doing.

If you have very limited time to reflect then there is a simple process that you can use where you ask only three questions:

1. **What?** Description stage – what happened?

---

[18] https://www.methodist.org.uk/our-faith/life-and-faith/the-methodist-modern-art-collection/resources/.

2. **So what?** Knowledge and understanding stage – so what does this tell me, teach me, help me understand, etc. and what theory and theology might help in getting that broader perspective?

3. **Now what?** Action stage – what have I learned that I need to apply, implement, think about, change etc.?[19]

Takeaways

- Be habitual in your theological reflection and use a variety of ways into reflection
- Always identify what difference doing the reflection has made
- Remember we can all do theology and theological reflection and that theological reflection will help us grow in our discipleship and be more effective in ministry
- Expect to be able to reflect in all sorts of settings from reading the Bible to watching the television or going for a walk
- Keep praying and expect insights

And on that note...

---

[19] Rolfe, G., Freshwater, D. & Jasper, M. (2001). *Critical Reflection for Nursing and the Helping Professions: a user's guide*. Palgrave: Basingstoke.

Our Prayer for You

May you know enough to know you know very little
And may that set you free from fear
And the need to control

May you embrace uncertainty
With humility and grace
And delight in the surprises that come your way

May you grow in knowledge and understanding
Continue to seek wisdom
And use your learning to liberate others

May you find joy in learning from those you set out to teach
And delight that in serving others
You too are blessed

May you flourish in this sacred vocation
Enjoy the adventure
And in it find deep joy

May your ministry draw you closer to God
May your ministry draw others closer to God
May God bless your ministry

Amen

Afterword

Our desire has been to try and play our part in helping to liberate Christian learning. In writing we have sought to equip the reader with a tool box to use, adapt and add to as they minister in the many varied and different contexts of teaching and learning in the church. We have tried to keep in mind grass roots community learning rather than more formal academic approaches, although much of what we have written still applies.

We recognise that when we facilitate teaching and learning, how we do it is as important as what is done. What is 'caught' is often more powerful than what is 'taught'. Who we are, our hopes, our values, our backgrounds all make a difference and have an influence on others. For example, we are aware that all three of us writing this book are white women who have been involved in theological education for many years. We have written from a particular perspective and position of privilege. We have our own gaps and blind spots.

We also want to acknowledge how much we have been influenced by and benefited from writers of black, feminist and liberation theology and transformative educational theory. If you are interested in doing more background reading we have added a 'Digging Deeper' list of thinkers who have influenced us personally, after the bibliography.

All of these are useful for critically examining our own and others' perspectives and practices, and for shedding light on the use and abuse of power in contexts of teaching and learning. We know ourselves how easy it is to fall out of consciousness of this and so we would like to suggest a few final questions to ponder before you decide to take on board a teaching or learning role in the church:

Why am I doing this role?

How much is it to boost my own ego?

What power will this role give me?

How can I stay aware of this?

What assumptions and beliefs do I bring to this role?

>About God?

>About learning?

About the potential learners?

>About myself?

>Who am I not thinking about?

What domains of privilege do I inhabit?

What do I hope to role model as a facilitator of teaching and learning?

What do I actually role model as a facilitator of teaching and learning?

Where is God in it?

What scriptures guide and inform my role as a facilitator of teaching and learning?

How do I keep myself rooted in God?

How and to whom am I accountable?

Appendices

Learning Checklist

Why?
What is the learning need and how does it fit in with the mission and ministry of God?
Whose is the learning need?
How has the learning need been identified and by whom?
How can this learning need be addressed?

What?
What are the aims and objectives of the learning?
What needs to be covered?
How does it need to be covered?
How is feedback going to be gathered?
How is the learning intervention going to be evaluated?

Who?
Who is this for?
How are they going to be invited?
Who is going to enable the learning?
What is their role? (e.g. facilitator, tutor, mentor, listener, lecturer)
Who else is going to support the learning?
What is their role? (e.g. host, refreshments, IT enabler)

Where?
Where is this going to take place, bearing in mind needs for confidentiality and safety?
Has venue risk analysis been done?
Has access been considered and addressed?

When?
What time has been chosen and for what reason?
Does this prevent some people from coming along who would like to be there?
What can be done about that?
How will feedback and evaluation be reviewed?
How will theological reflection be formally embedded in the timetable?
Has the person enabling the learning got the time to prepare and reflect?

Example Learning Checklist

Why?
What is the learning need and how does it fit in with the mission and ministry of God? *The need is for deeper understanding for discipleship. This fits with the second mark of mission, to teach, baptize and nurture new believers.*
Whose is the learning need? *A group of new Christians who have just completed an Alpha course. However, there is also a more general demand for more in-depth learning about faith.*
How has the learning need been identified and by whom? *The participants of the course were asked what they would like to learn next by the facilitator.*
How can this this learning need be addressed? *It is very important to meet their desire to learn and expand their understanding. After further consultation it was decided to explore scripture and to create a short series to introduce Mark's gospel.*

What?
What are the aims and objectives of the learning? *To deepen understanding of Mark's Gospel and to give confidence to the learners that they have a grasp of an account of Jesus' life, ministry, death and resurrection.*
What needs to be covered? It was decided to begin with an overview, and then explore both specific themes and different ways of approaching.
How does it need to be covered? *Mixed teaching methods are needed to appeal to different learner preferences.*
How is feedback going to be gathered? Group discussion in class and written feedback.

How is the learning intervention going to be evaluated? *Feedback will be asked for after each session. At the end of the series learners will also be asked what difference the teaching has made to them in terms of faith and how they live their lives.*

Who?

Who is this for? *The group identified above but it will also be open to anyone else who would like to learn.*

How are they going to be invited? *The new course will be advertised through notices, word of mouth, personal invitation, newsletter, social media, poster.*

Who is going to enable the learning? *The new curate. Although they have no previous experience of facilitating learning, this is seen as a learning opportunity for them too.*

What is their role? (e.g. facilitator, tutor, mentor, listener, lecturer.) *Learning facilitator.*

Who else is going to support the learning? *A Reader, who is an experienced educator, and who will in turn be supervised.*

What is their role? (e.g. host, refreshments, IT enabler) *Their principal role is mentor to the learning facilitator. However, they will also be on standby to assist during the sessions and occasionally demonstrate co-facilitation.*

Where?

Where is this going to take place, bearing in mind needs for confidentiality and safety? *The Church Hall meeting room. The room is warm and friendly, with safety glass doors and good facilities for refreshments.*

Has venue risk analysis been done? *Yes. The hall has regular risk assessments.*

Has access been considered and addressed? *Yes. There is full disabled access and facilities, including a hearing loop.*

When?

What time has been chosen and for what reason? *6.30pm Friday to coincide with Youth Club so that parents can attend whilst waiting for their children.*

Does this prevent some people from coming along who would like to be there? *Yes. There are people who do not like coming out in the evening, and others who cannot because of other care commitments.*

What can be done about that? *It was decided to offer a repeat session on Wednesday lunchtime.*

How will feedback and evaluation be reviewed? *There will be an informal review meeting between the learning facilitator and mentor after each session using TEAM and PEE. A further, more formal, review will be held at the end of the course.*

How will theological reflection be formally embedded in the timetable? *This will be included at the end of each session and again at the end of the course.*

Has the person enabling the learning got the time to prepare and reflect? *Yes.*

Example Teaching Session Outlines

Session 1	Materials	Methods	Time
Opening Prayer			5 minutes
Introductions	Ice Breaker	Group exercise	5 minutes
	Individual input	Explore previous learning and hopes for new learning	20 minutes
Overview of Mark's Gospel – Where, when, how, etc. Key themes, theology, characters, places and events	PowerPoint – including sources for further exploration	Talk	20 minutes
	Discussion of presentation	In pairs, then feedback to group + Q & A	10 minutes
Break			15 minutes
Ways of approaching the text	Bible – individual	Silent reading	10 minutes
	Bible – group	Dramatic reading	10 minutes
	Recording or podcast	Sing song together based on the text	10 minutes
	Art work	Meditation	10 minutes

Session 1	Materials	Methods	Time
Closing prayer			5 minutes

Session 2	Materials	Methods	Time
Opening Prayer			5 minutes
Ways of encountering text	Bible	Lectio divina	25 minutes
Different ways of reading the Bible – literal / instruction / proof texts / history / devotion and prayer / wisdom for living	Cards with brief explanations on tables	Apply to a situation of their choice	15 minutes
		Group feedback	15 minutes
Break			15 minutes
Reflections on learning so far	Sticky notes and white boards	Ask to record key learning points / questions raised / what found surprising / anything else	40 minutes
Closing Prayer			5 minutes

Session 3	Materials	Methods	Time
Opening Prayer			5 minutes
Relating the text to today	Newspapers	Work in small groups to find a text in Mark and apply it to an article	25 minutes
		Feedback to Group	10 minutes
		Group discussion about the benefits and dangers of using the text to guide day to day life	20 minutes
Break			15 minutes
So what?	PowerPoint	Introduction to 5 Marks of Mission	5 minutes
		In five groups discuss how a mark of mission might be pursued in response to Mark's Gospel	30 minutes
Closing prayer	To include intentions following learning		10 minutes

Bibliography

Buechner, F. (1993). *Wishful Thinking: a seeker's ABC.* San Francisco, CA: HarperSanFrancisco, p. 144.

Daines, J., Daines, C., & Graham, B. (1993). *Adult Learning, Adult Teaching.* University of Nottingham.

Fleming, N. D. (1995, July). 'I'm different; not dumb. Modes of presentation (VARK) in the tertiary classroom.' In *Research and development in higher education, Proceedings of the 1995 Annual Conference of the Higher Education and Research Development Society of Australasia (HERDSA), HERDSA* (Vol. 18, pp. 308-313).

Fowler, J. W. (1981). *Stages of Faith: the psychology of human development.* San Francisco, CA: Harper & Row.

Gardner, H. E. (2000). *Intelligence Reframed: multiple intelligences for the 21st century.* Hachette UK.

Gilligan, C. (1993). *In a Different Voice: psychological theory and women's development.* Harvard University Press.

Grave Talk (2015). London: Church House Publishing.

Green, L. (1990). *Let's Do Theology: a pastoral cycle resource book.* London: Continuum.

Honey, P., & Mumford, A. (1989). *Learning Styles Questionnaire.* Organization Design and Development, Incorporated.

Kirkpatrick, J. D. & Kirkpatrick, W. K. (2016). *Kirkpatrick's Four Levels of Training Evaluation.* Association for Talent Development.

Knight, Rhona. 'Giving and receiving feedback'. In Hastings, A. & Redsell, S. (eds.) (2006). *The Good Consultation Guide for Nurses.* Abingdon: Radcliffe Publishing.

Knowles, M. S., Holton III, E. F., Swanson, R. A., & Robinson, P. A. (2020). *The Adult Learner: the definitive classic in adult education and human resource development.* London: Routledge.

Kolb, D. A. (2007). *The Kolb Learning Style Inventory.* Boston, MA: Hay Resources Direct.

Kushner, L. (1977). *Honey from the Rock: Visions of Jewish Mystical Renewal*. New York: Harper and Row.

Mallison, J. (1997). *The Small Group Leader*. London: Scripture Union.

McCarthy, B., & McCarthy, D. (2006). *Teaching around the 4MAT® cycle: Designing instruction for diverse learners with diverse learning styles*. Thousand Oaks, CA: Corwin Press.

Nash, S. & Nash, P. (2006). *Tools for Reflective Ministry*. London: SPCK.

Rolfe, G., Freshwater, D. & Jasper, M. (2001). *Critical Reflection for Nursing and the Helping Professions: a user's guide*. Palgrave: Basingstoke.

Slee, N. (2004). *Women's Faith Development: patterns and processes*. Aldershot: Ashgate.

Streib, H. (2001). 'Faith development theory revisited: The religious styles perspective.' *The International Journal for the Psychology of Religion*, 11(3), 143-158.

Tuckman, B. W. (1965). 'Developmental sequence in small groups.' *Psychological Bulletin*, 63(6), 384-399.

Westerhoff III, J. H. (1976). *Will Our Children Have Faith?* New York, NY: Seabury.

Digging Deeper

Belenky, M. F., Clinchy, B. M., Goldberger, N. R., & Tarule, J. M. (1986). *Women's Ways of Knowing: The development of self, voice, and mind*. New York: Basic Books.

Bruner, J. (1996). *The Culture of Education*. Cambridge, MA: Harvard University Press.

Bruner, J. S. (2009). *Actual Minds, Possible Worlds*. Cambridge, MA: Harvard University Press.

Christ, C. P. (2015). *Diving Deep & Surfacing: Women writers on spiritual quest*. Beacon Press.

Freire, P. (2000). *Pedagogy of the Oppressed*. New York: Continuum.

Freire, P. (2015). *Pedagogy of Indignation*. Abingdon: Routledge.

hooks, b. (2013). *Teaching Community: A pedagogy of hope*. Routledge.

hooks, b. (2014). *Teaching to Transgress*. Abingdon: Routledge.

Mezirow, J. (2000). *Learning as Transformation: Critical Perspectives on a Theory in Progress.* The Jossey-Bass Higher and Adult Education Series. San Francisco: Jossey-Bass Publishers.

Moore, M. E. M. (2004). *Teaching as a Sacramental Act*. Cleveland: The Pilgrim Press.

Reddie, A. G. (2005). *Acting in Solidarity: Reflections in Critical Christianity*. London: DLT.

Shaw, P. (2014). *Transforming Theological Education*. Carlisle: Langham Partnership.

List of Bible References

Index

Comments on 'Liberating Christian Learning'

"This book will be an incredible tool for anyone involved in teaching or creating a learning environment for adults. It is packed with helpful tips and tools – exploring everything from the environment in which people might be learning through to their motivations for being there. Particularly helpful are the regular questions, inviting readers to consider their own setting and their own motives for teaching and sharing a learning space with others. This isn't so much a book to read as a handbook to guide your thinking from that initial thought through to running / hosting a course or Bible study. Brimming with wisdom and the experience that comes with years of practice, I heartily recommend this book for all trainers, teachers and those with a passion for learning."
Ali Campbell, Youth and Children's Ministry Consultant

"This book sets out exactly how to take any material and turn it into lively, engaging and effective training. It is ideal for who have to deliver training in their roles, but also has plenty of new ideas for people who have been training for years. A 'must-have' book for all trainers, both new and experienced"
Jennie Fytche, Trainer, mentor and coach

"A remarkably compact and accessible resource for all those engaged in Christian education, discipleship and mission. Theories, questions for self-reflection and case studies have been skilfully interwoven to take the reader through different stages of planning and preparing to teach in a Christian context. Well worth a read!"
Dr Alison Gray Director of Studies Tutor in Old Testament Language, Literature & Theology, Westminster College Cambridge

"A substantial yet accessible resource for all leaders and facilitators of Christian education in all contexts. It would especially appeal to anyone who values the distinctiveness of designing programmes, delivering courses, or learning, as Christians. Thank you Knight, Myers, and Nash for this well-researched guide, packed with practical, inspiring, and useful illustrations."

Revd Canon Eileen Harrop, Honorary Canon of Pilgrimage and of Durham Cathedral and Vice-Chair, Anglican Minority Ethnic Network (AMEN)

"This is a great resource for those called upon to help others learn. It won't tell you exactly what to do – it's not that kind of book. Instead, it will ask you lots of questions, point you to lots of resources, and help you imagine Christian learning in lots of exciting new ways. Whatever level and kind of learning you are involved in, you will find something to inspire you here."

Mike Higton, Professor of Theology and Ministry, Durham University

"Learning and teaching is an essential ingredients of Christian discipleship. However, Western protestant Christianity, a scriptural tradition shackled with enlightenment rationalism, has often confined learning to either the four walls of the academy or in between the leather-bound covers of inaccessible books. *Liberating Christian Learning* is an excellent resource that initiates a process of unshackling through sharing of experience and enabling the reader to find their own models and methods of learning and teaching."

Revd Shemil Mathew, Vice Dean of Emmanuel Theological College

"The contemporary crisis in lay discipleship has been one related to the paucity of adult Christian learning within the church. *Liberating Christian Learning* is an excellent resource that seeks to respond to this crisis by offering a range of resources and opportunities for facilitating reflection on experience that can break this historic log jam. *Liberating Christian Learning* does exactly what it says on the tin. Its excellence speaks for itself."

Professor Anthony G. Reddie, Director of the Oxford Centre for Religion and Culture, Regent's Park College, University of Oxford and Extraordinary Professor of Theological Ethics with the University of South Africa

Notes:

Notes:

Notes:

Notes:

Notes:

Printed in Great Britain
by Amazon

18873872R00078